BRAIN BLAST PUZZLES

Mazes Books for Adults

ActivityCrusades

Published by Speedy Publishing Canada Limited

ActivityCrusades
activity books

1

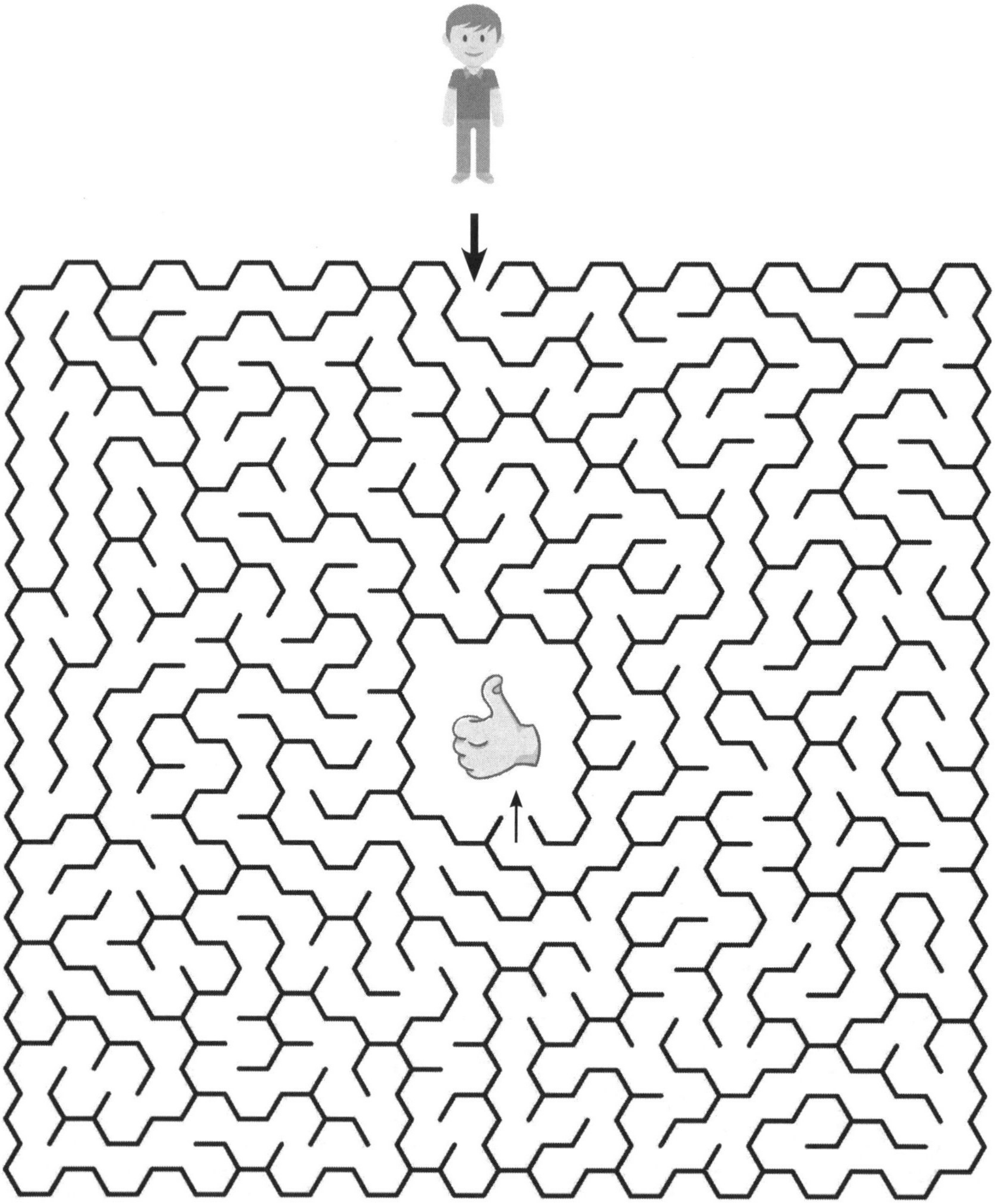

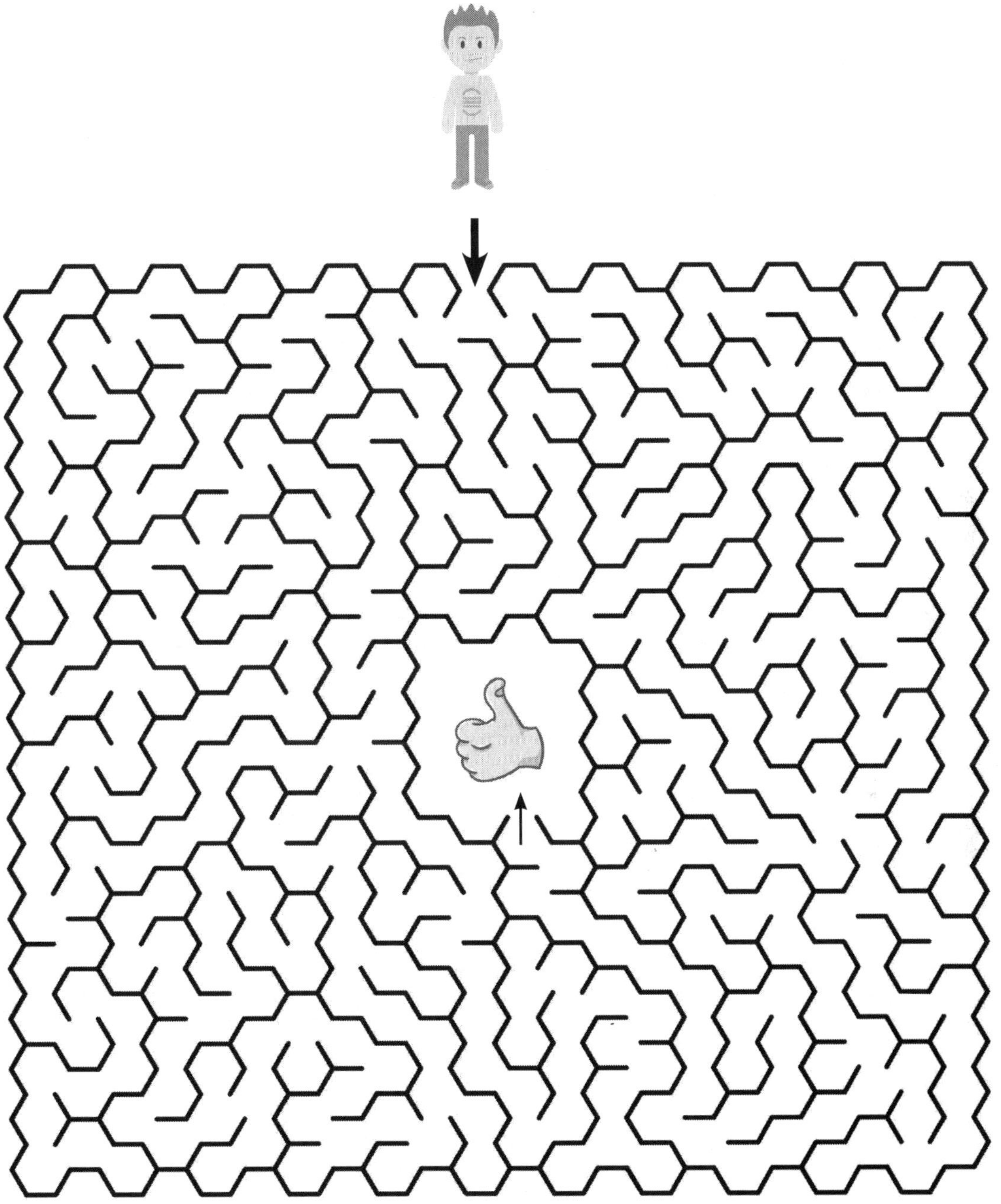

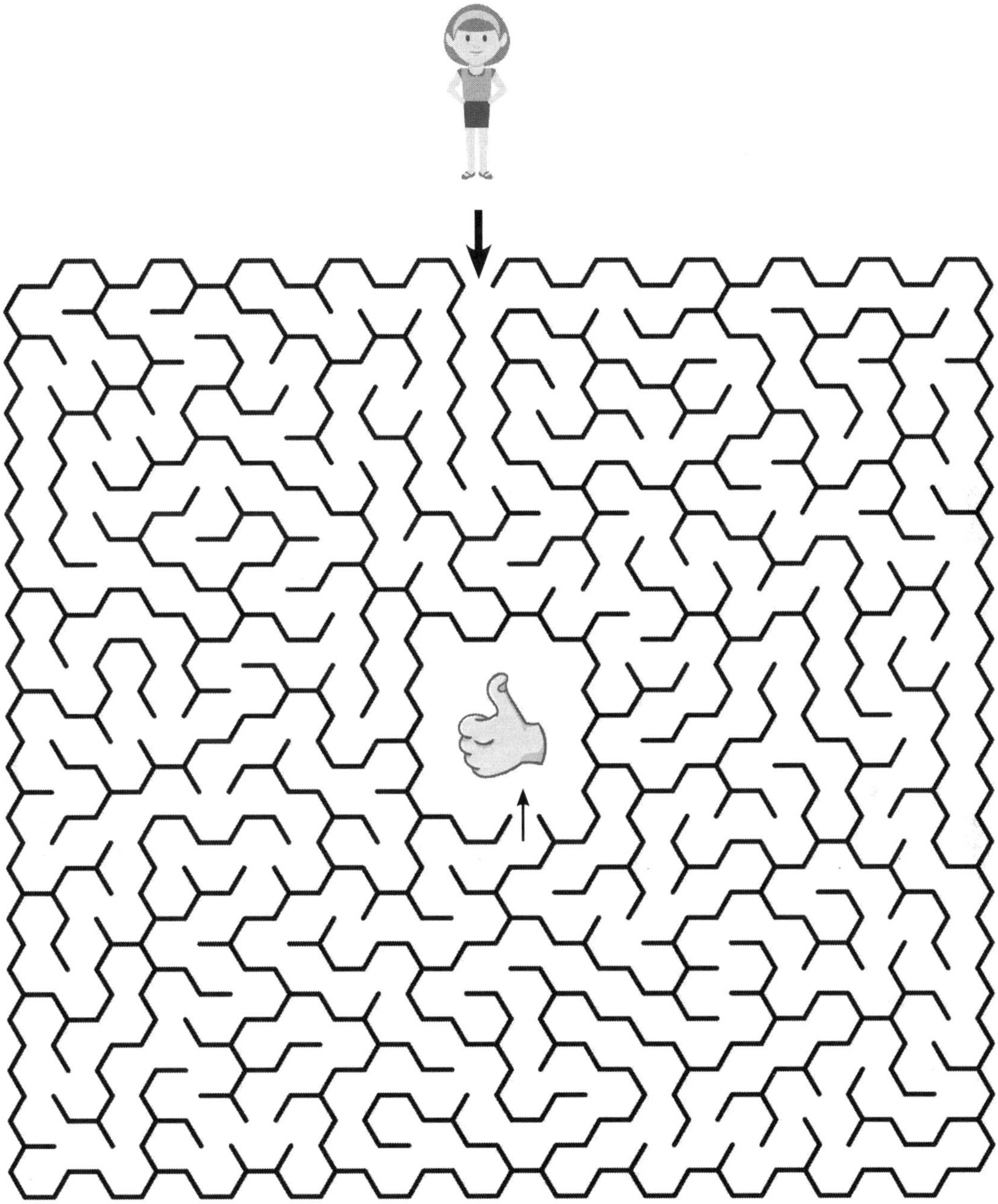

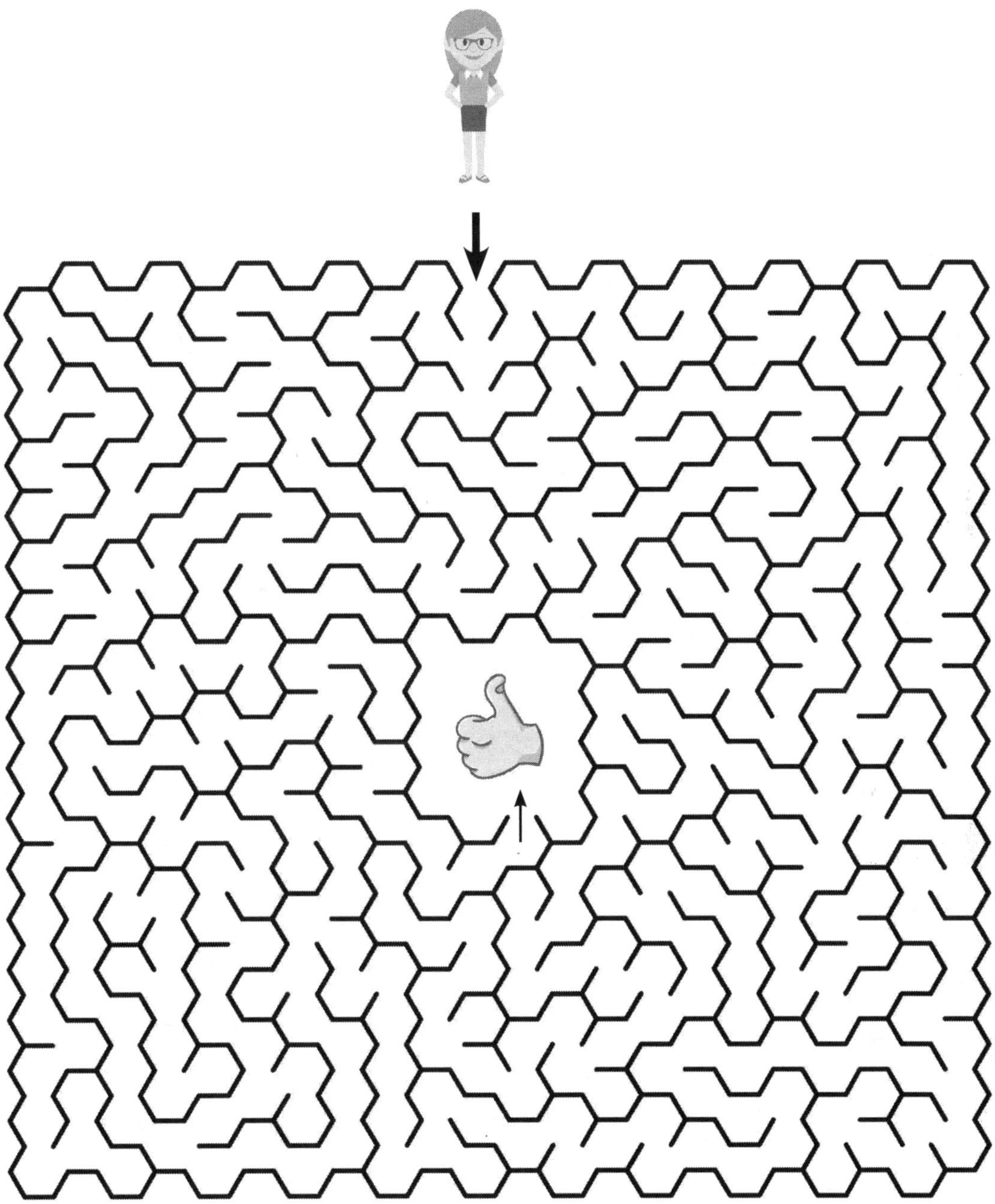

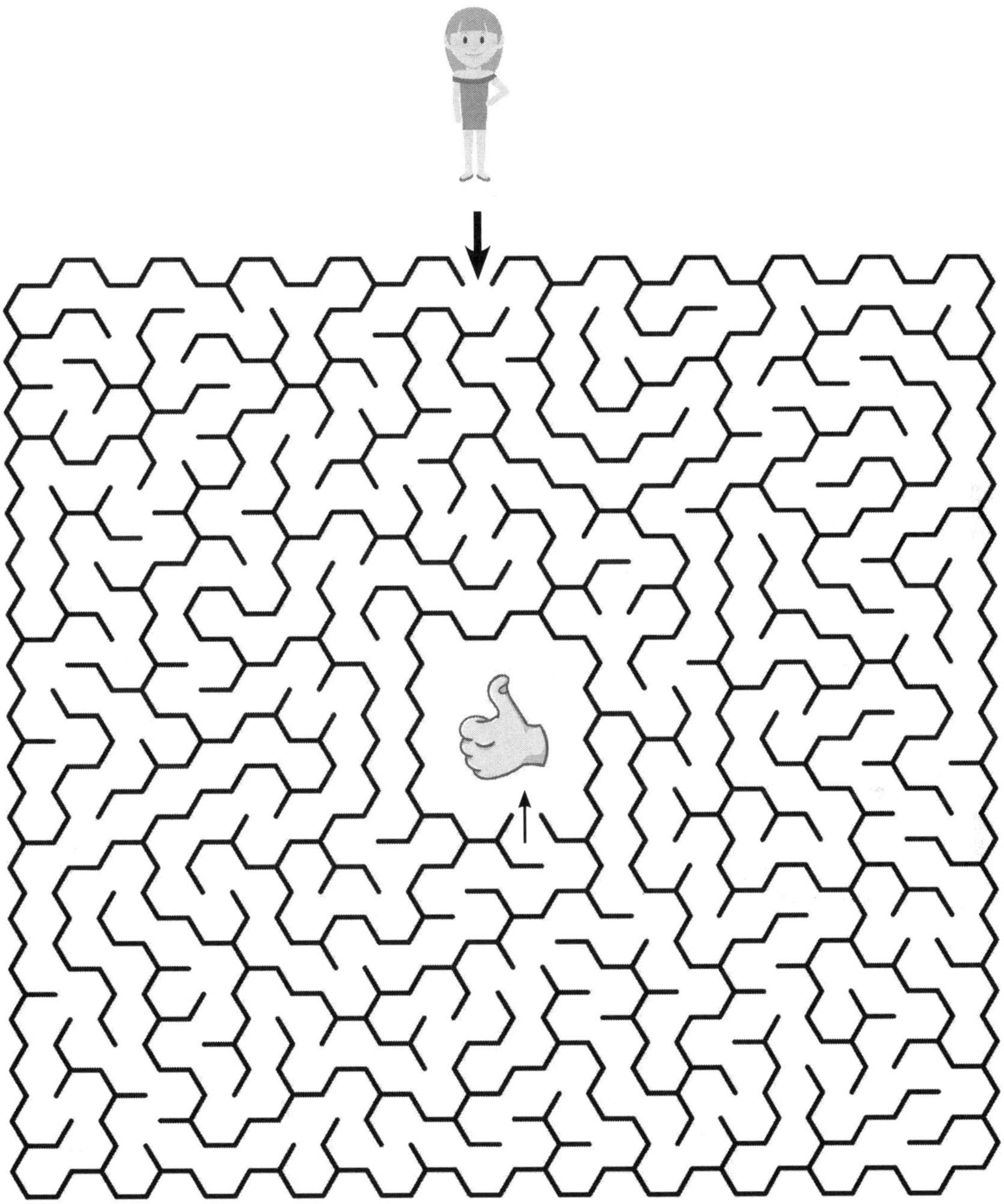

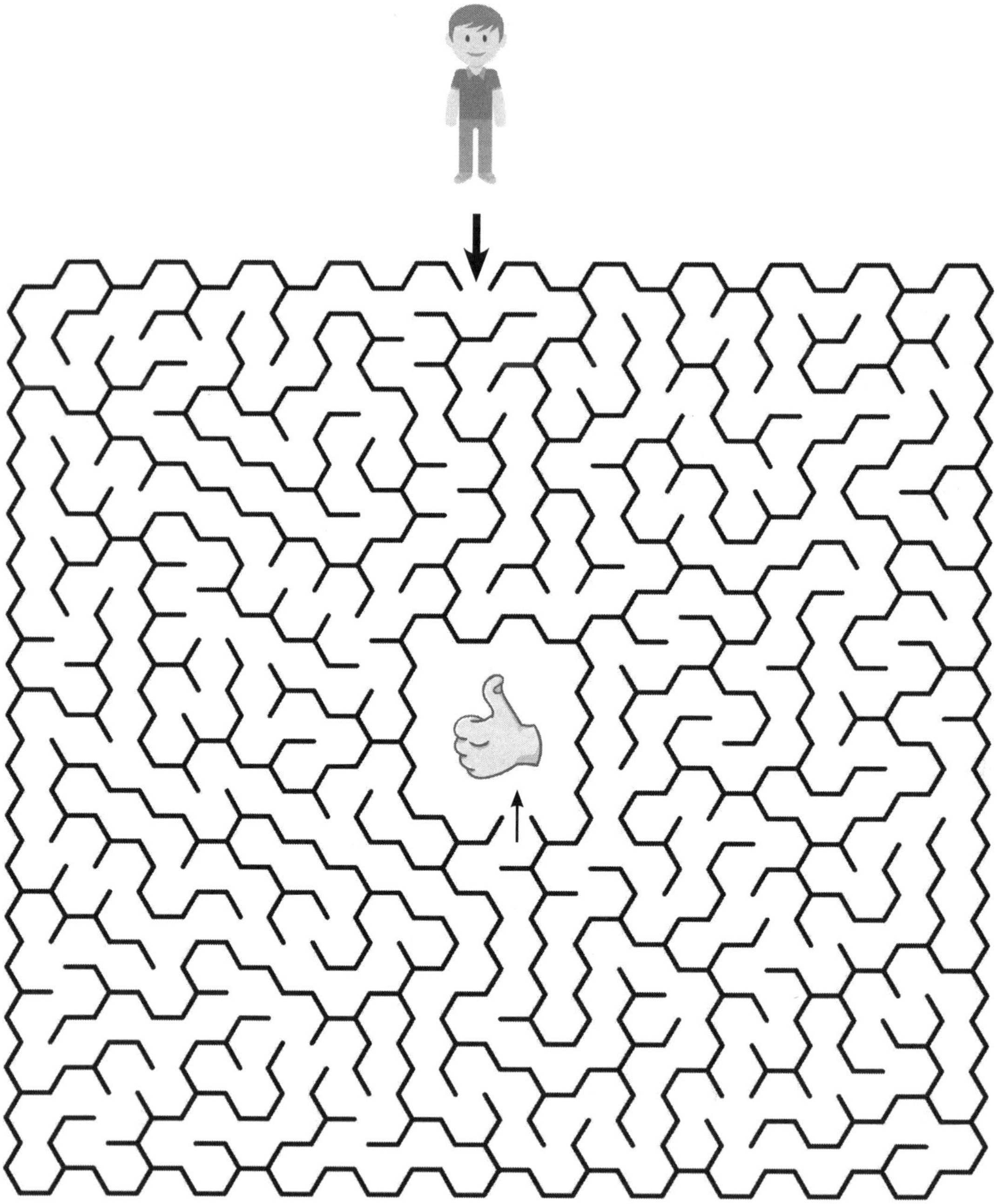

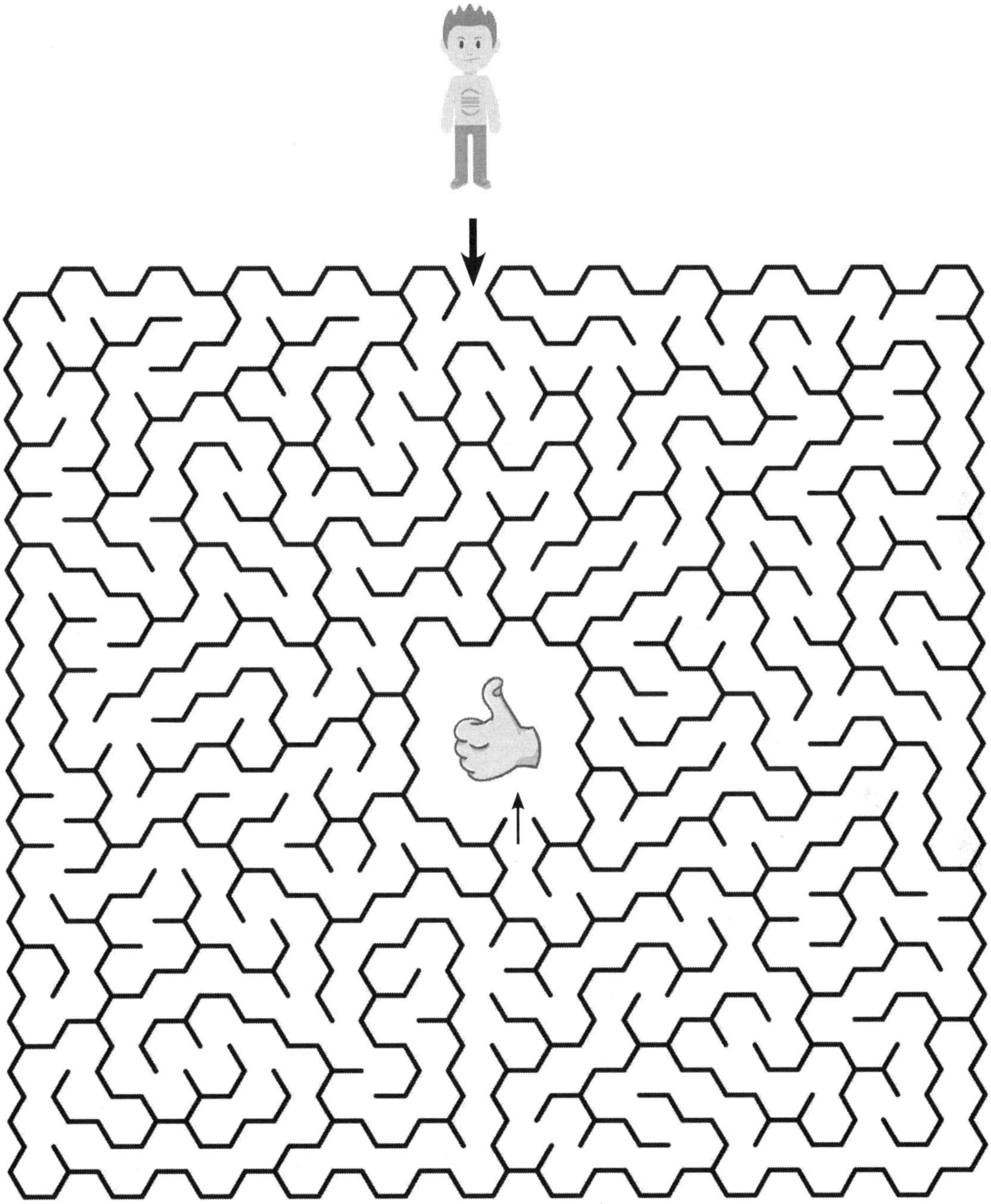

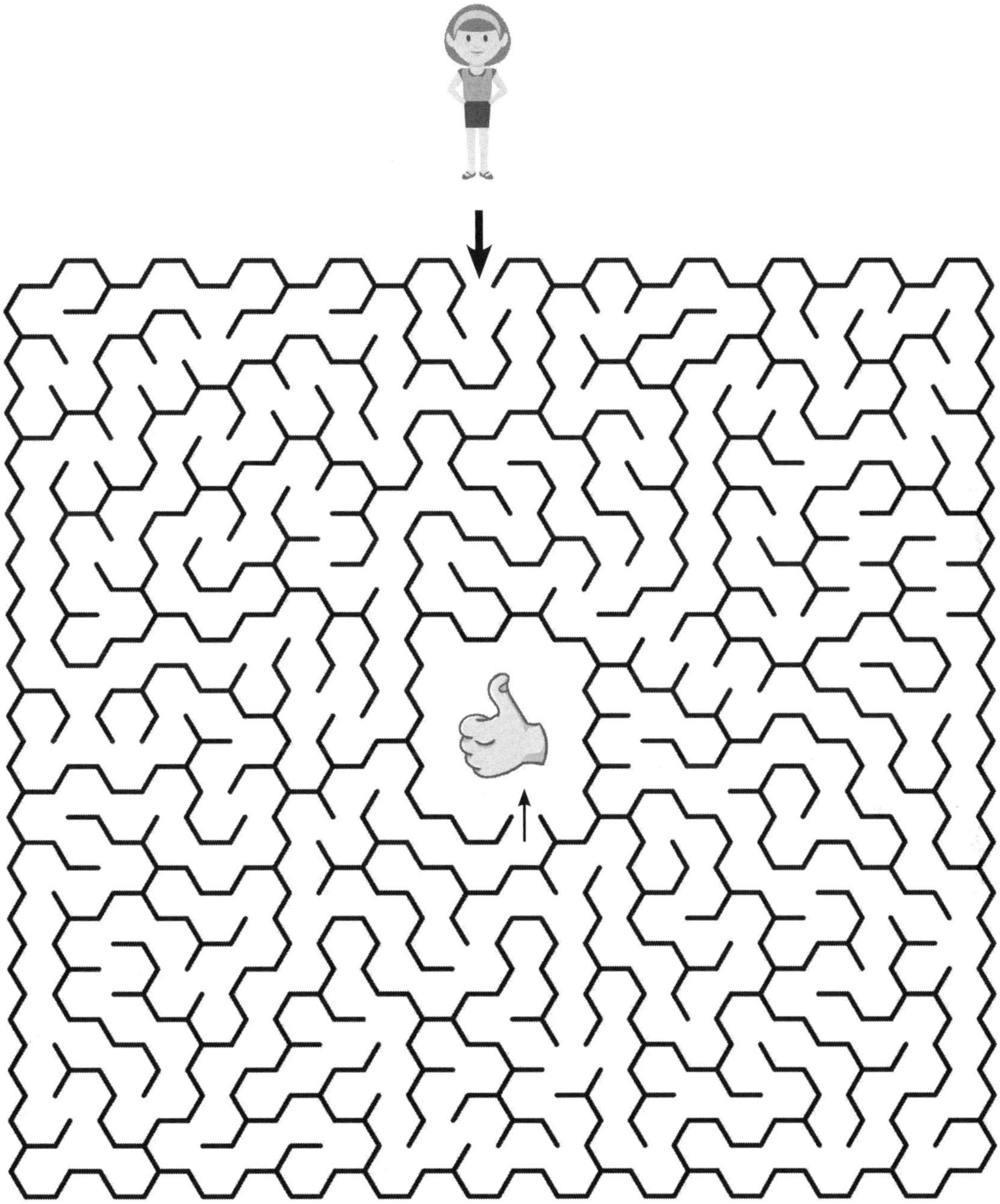

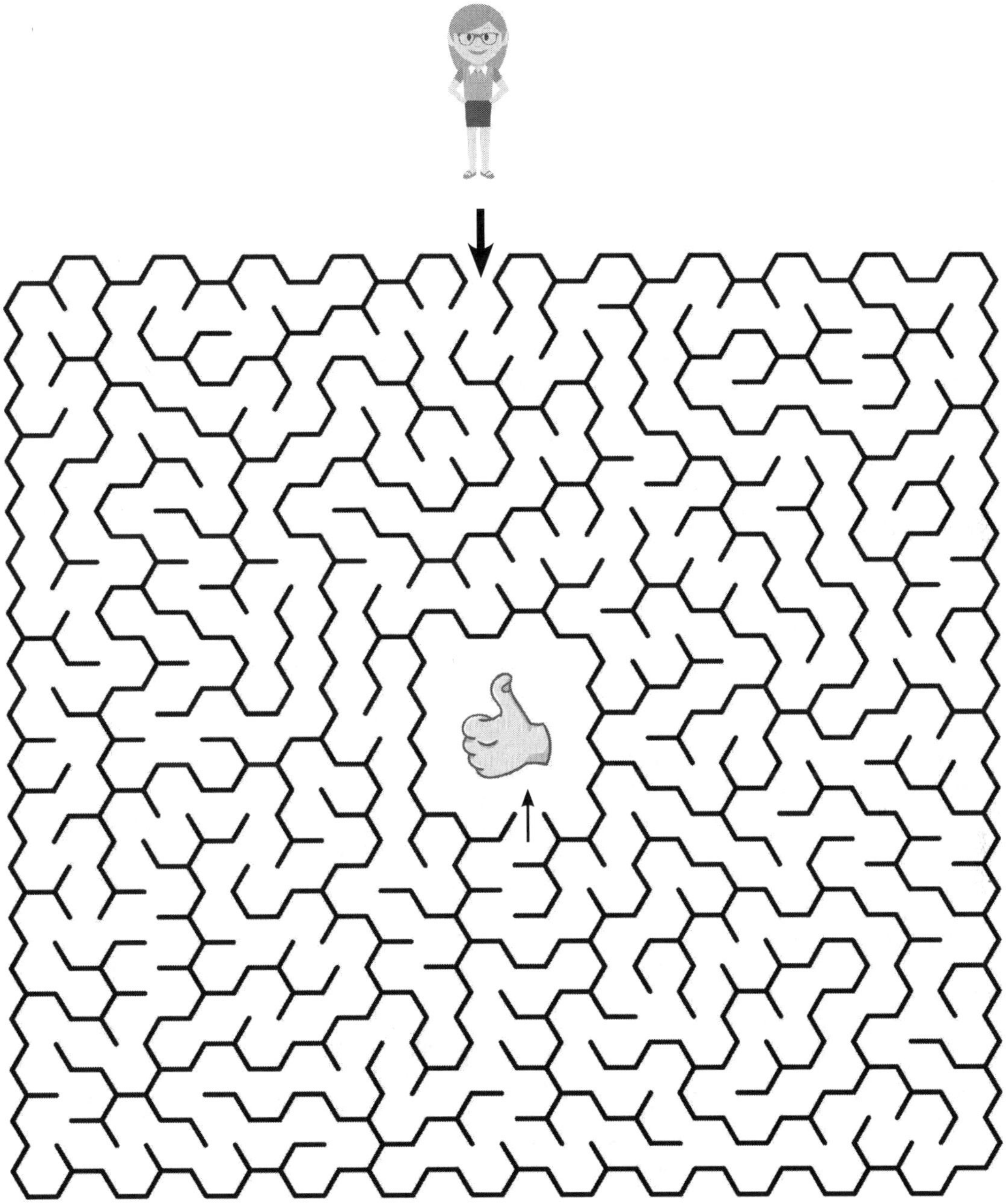

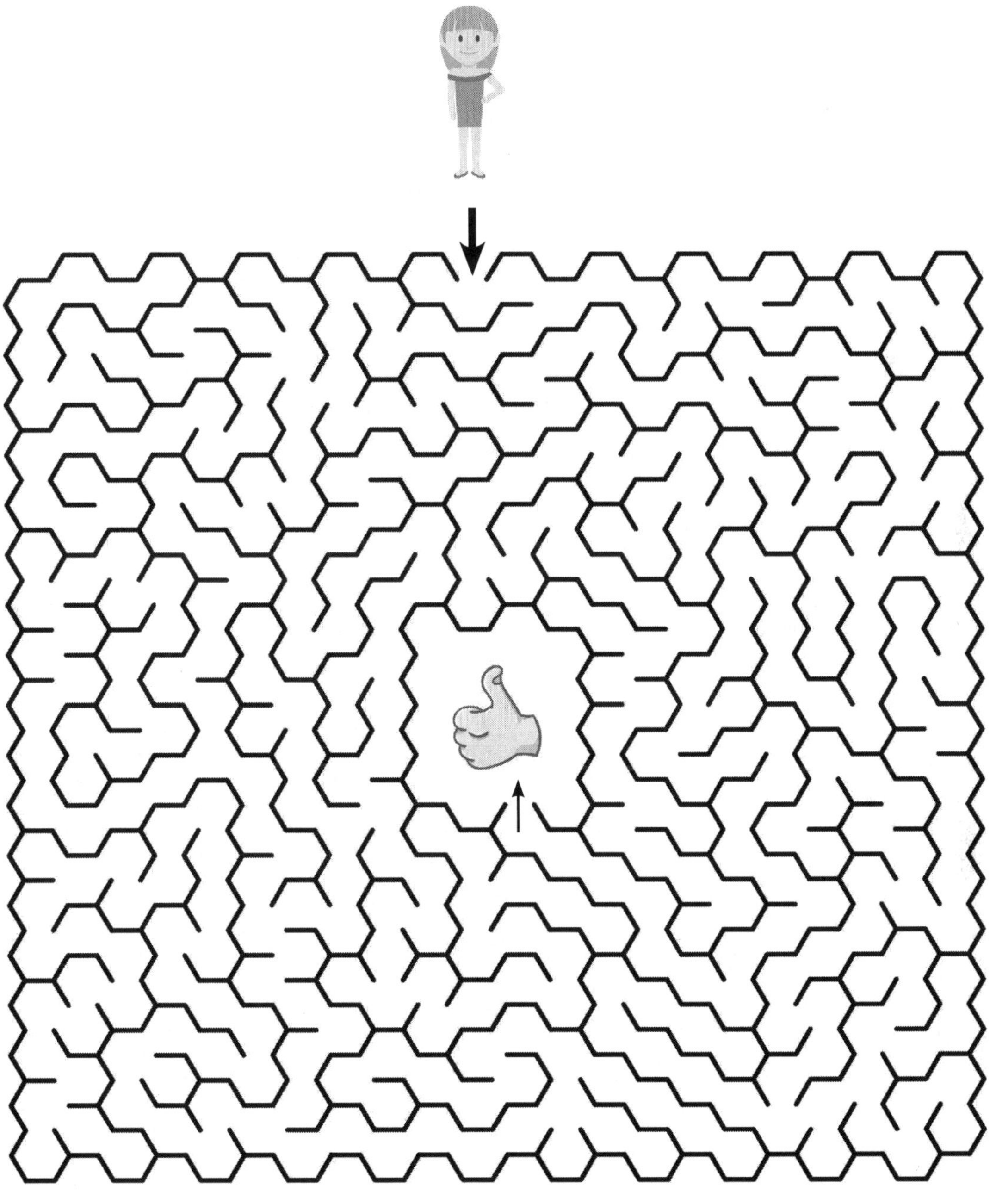

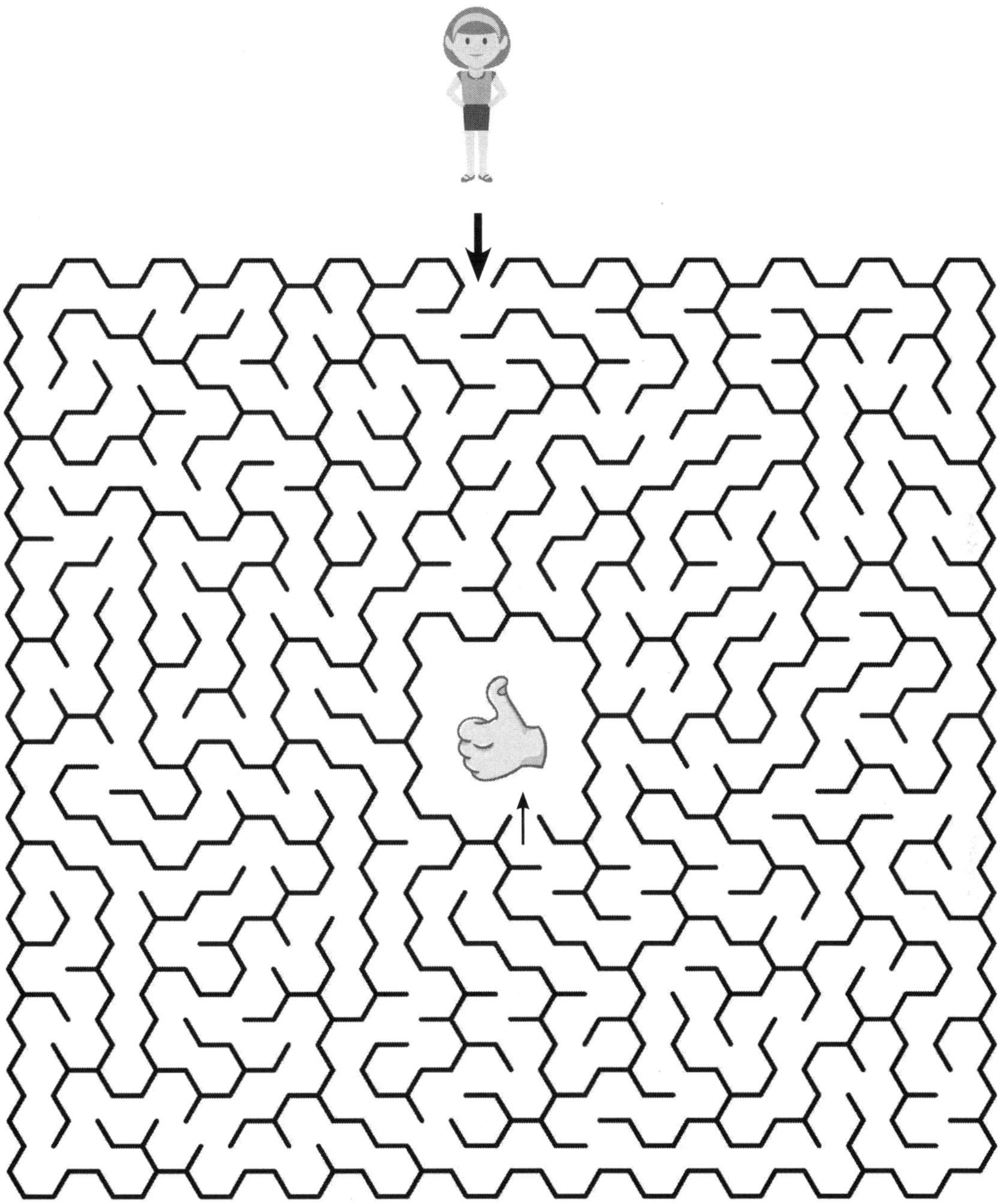

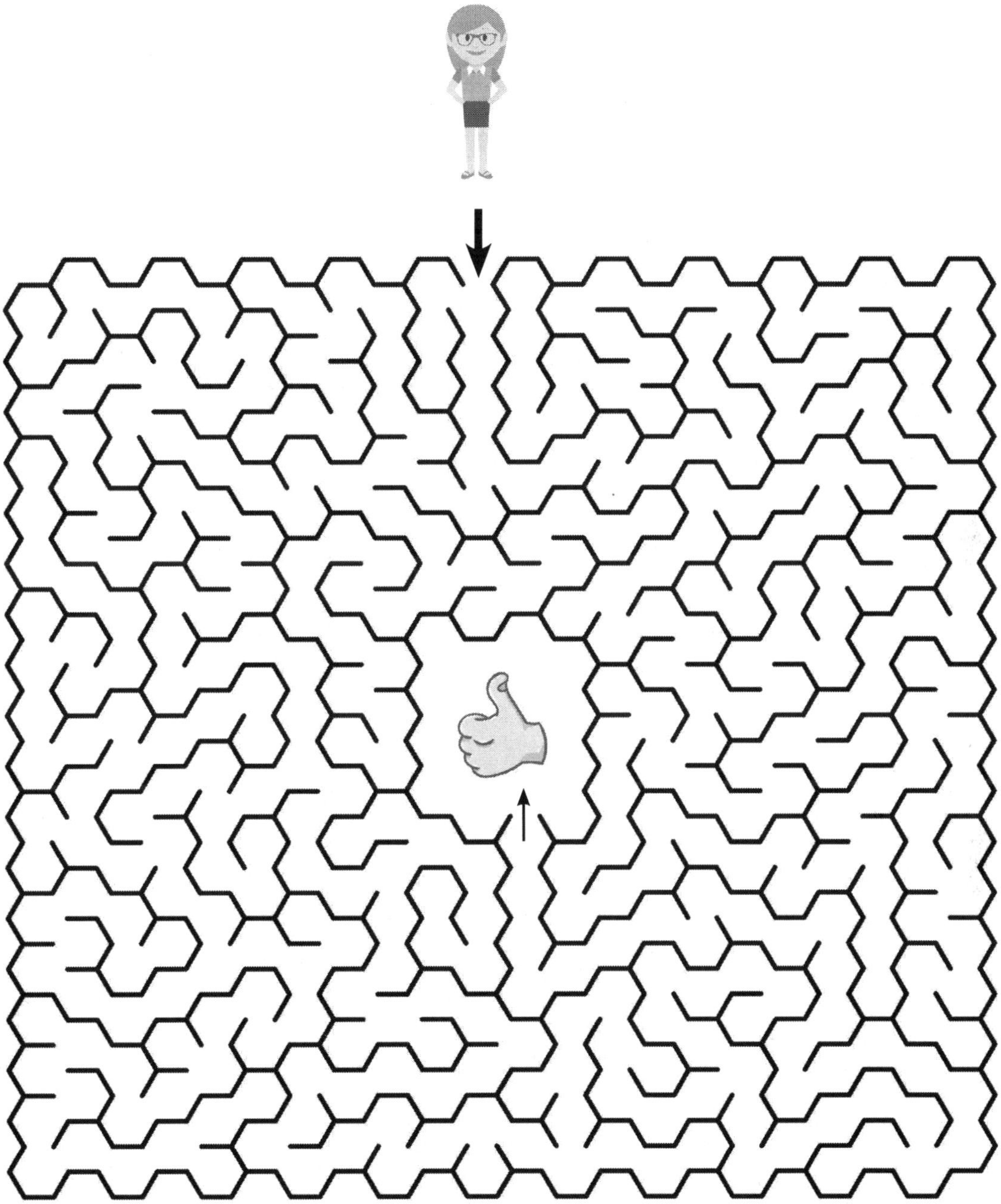

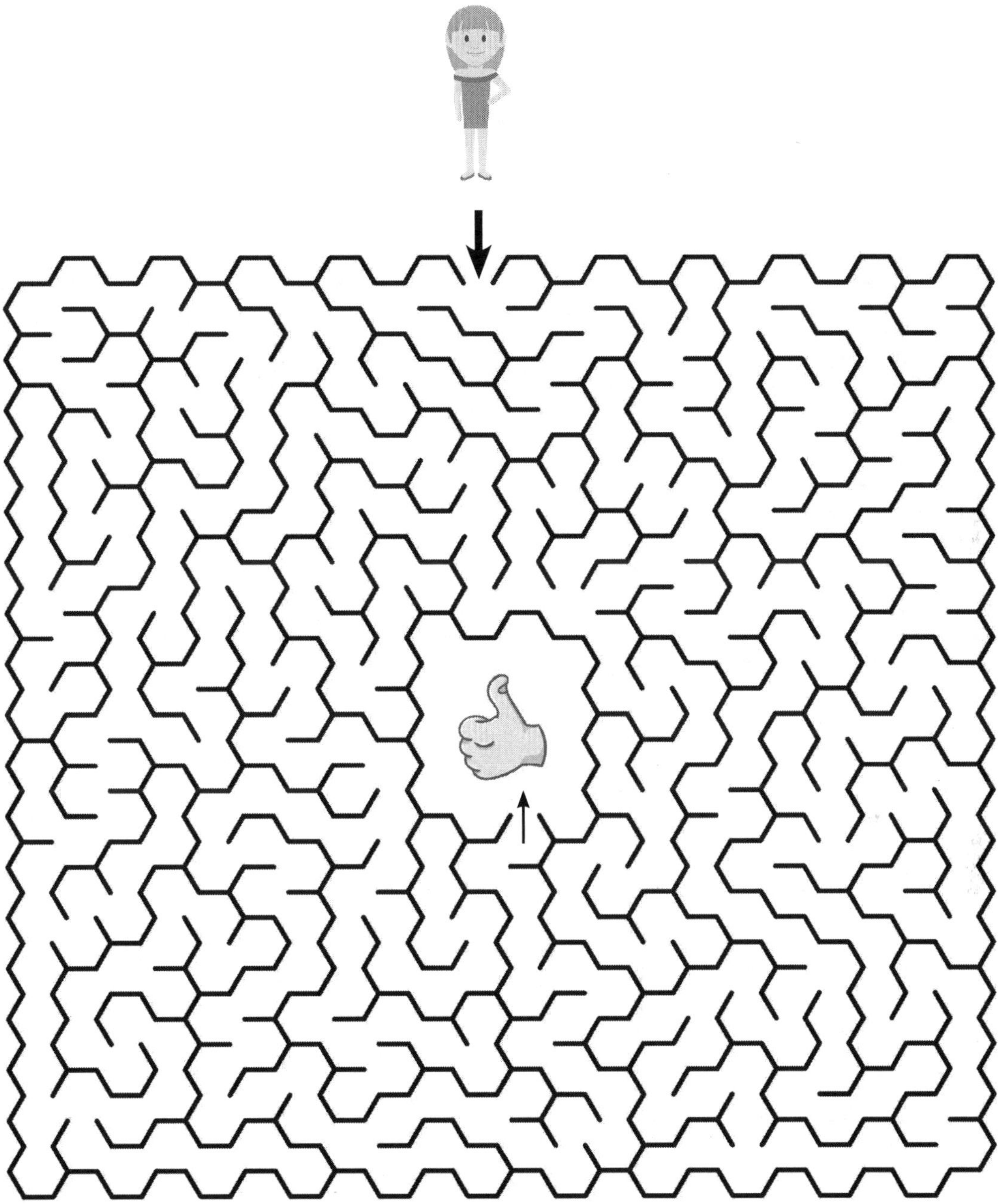

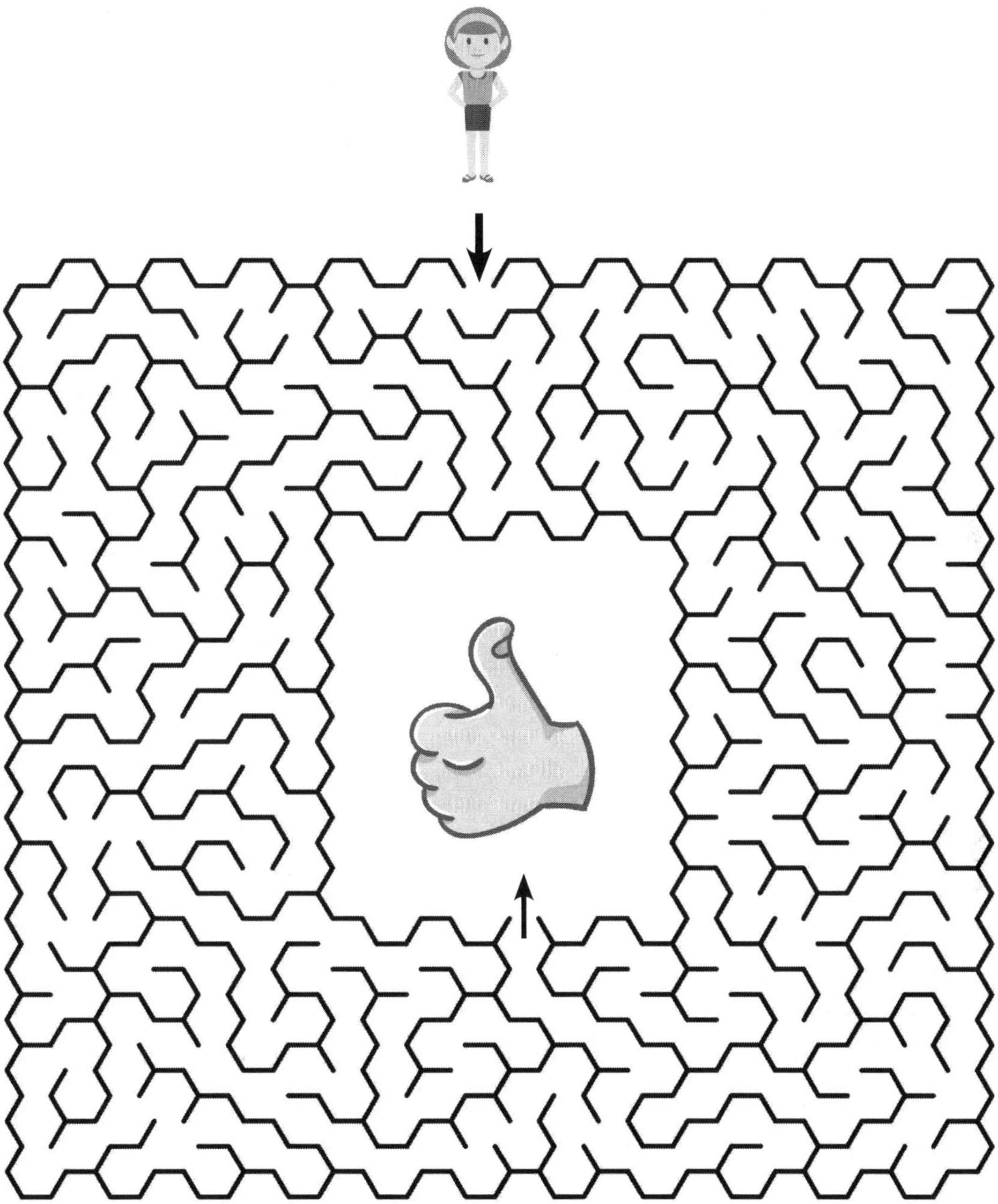

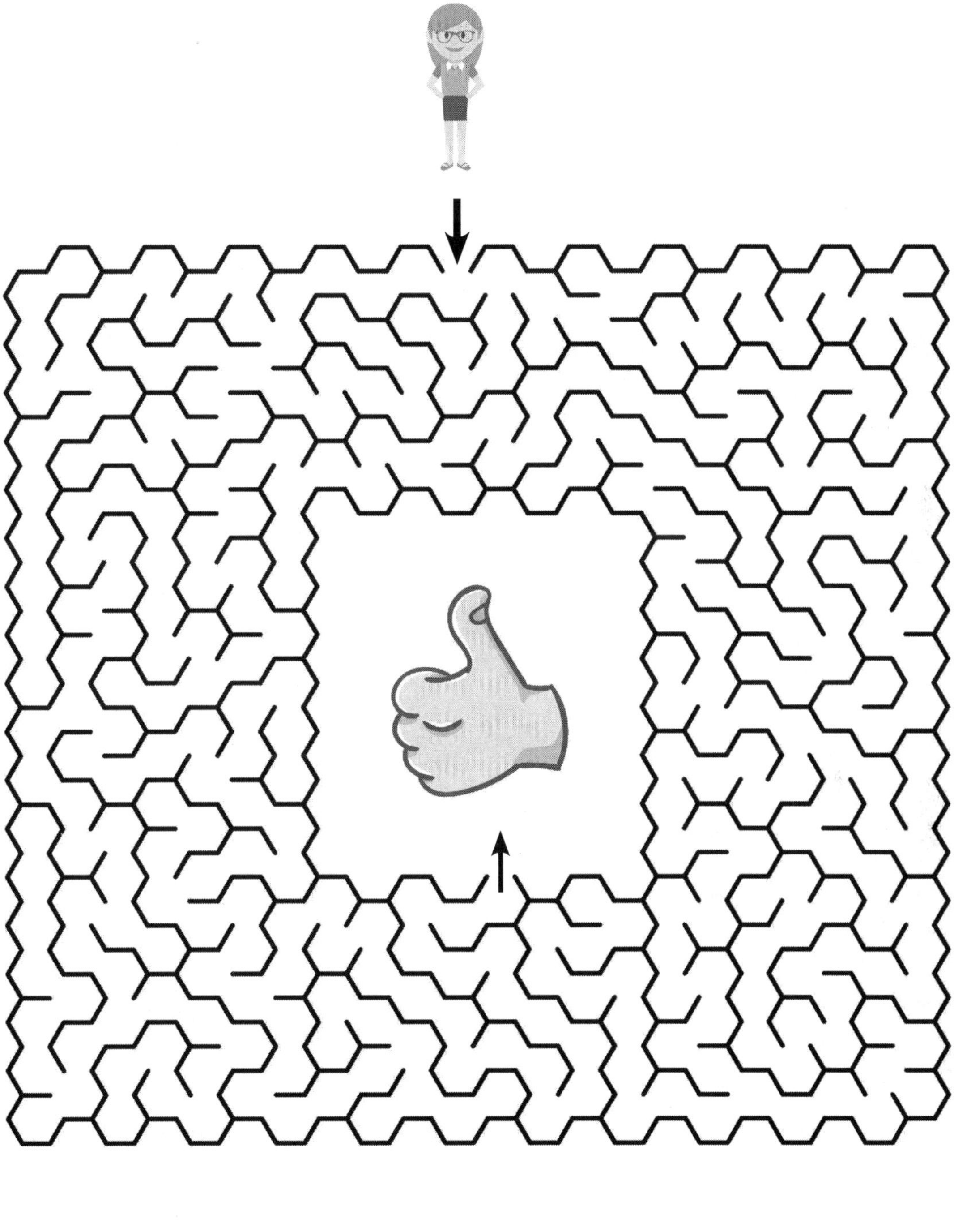

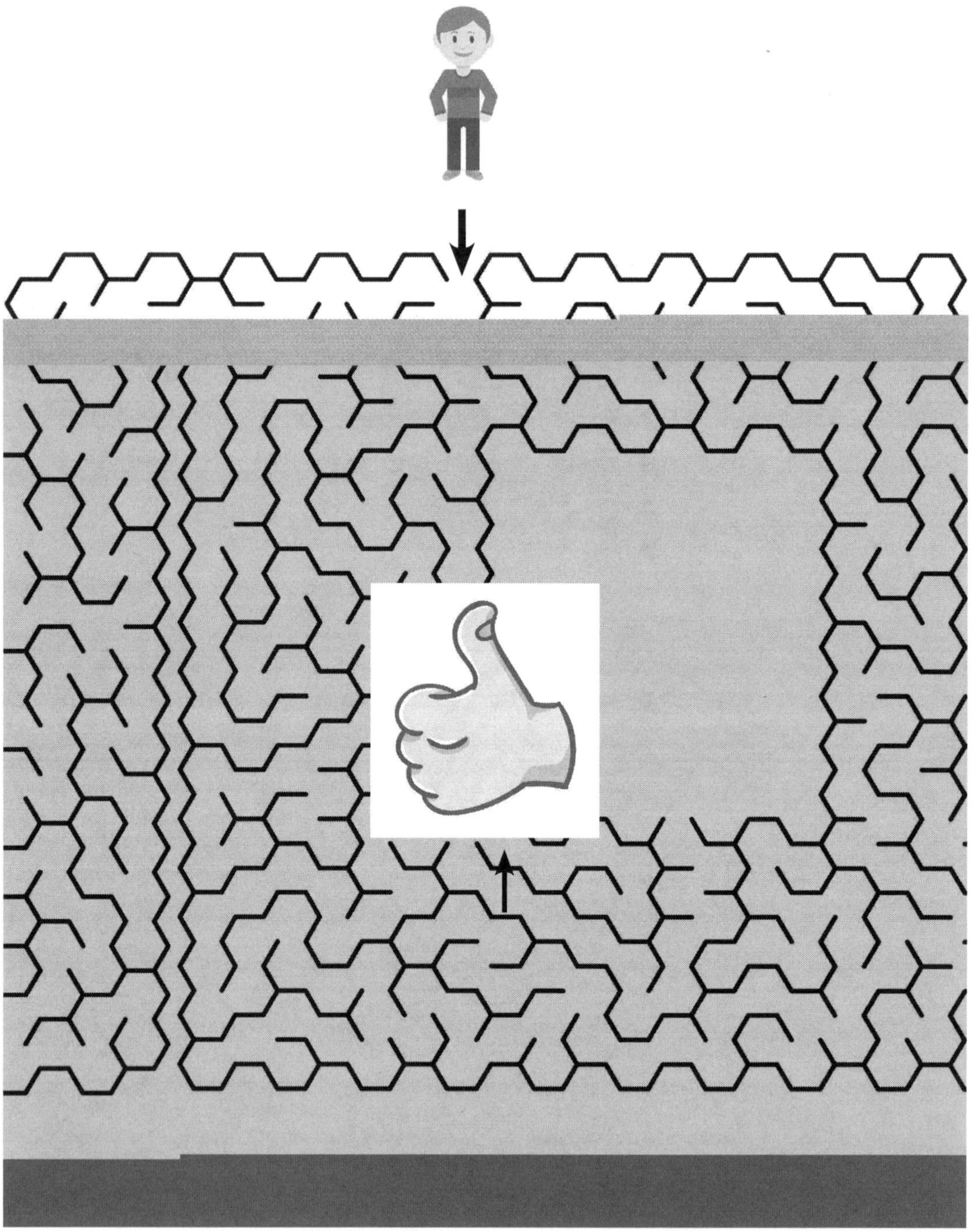

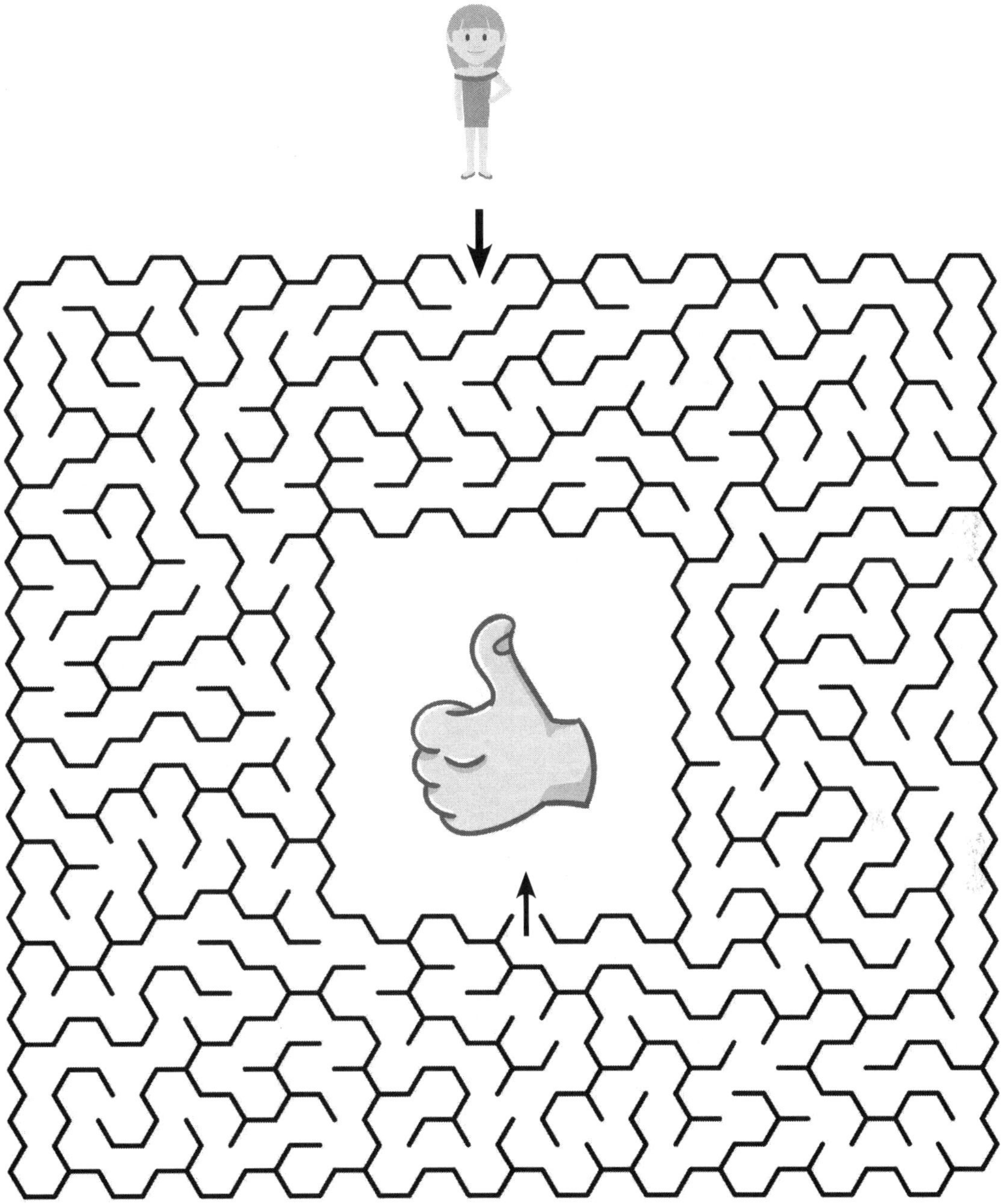

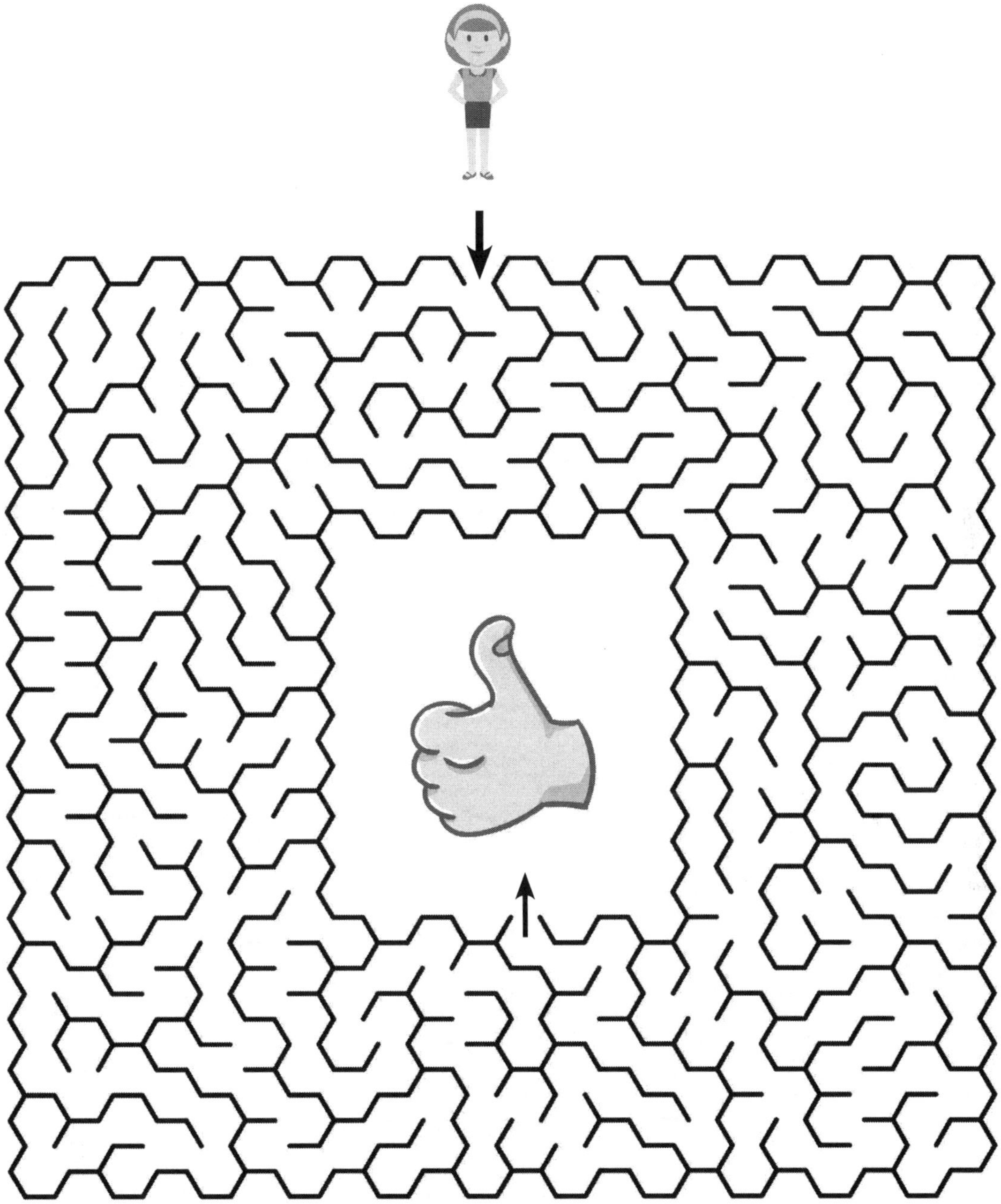

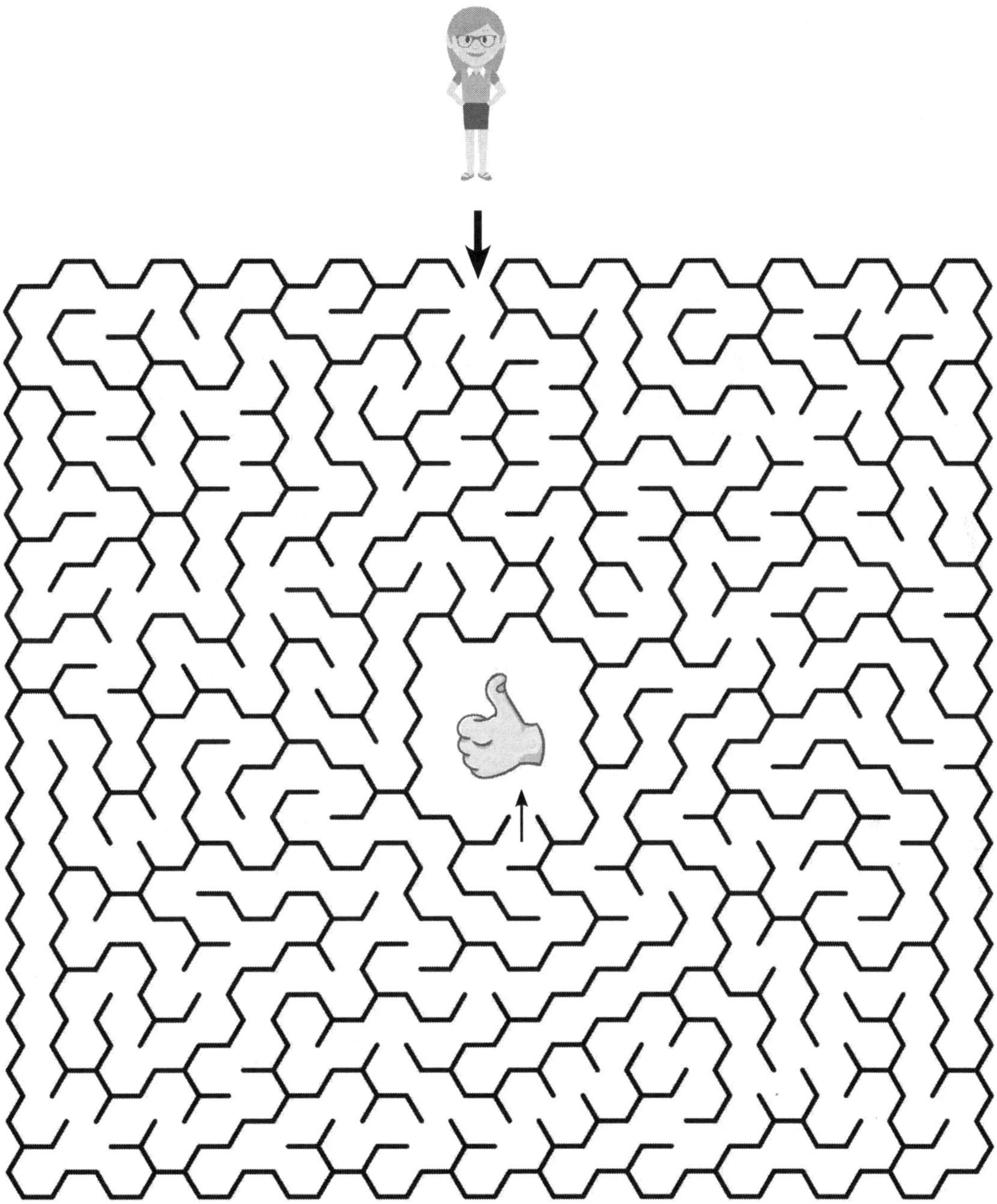

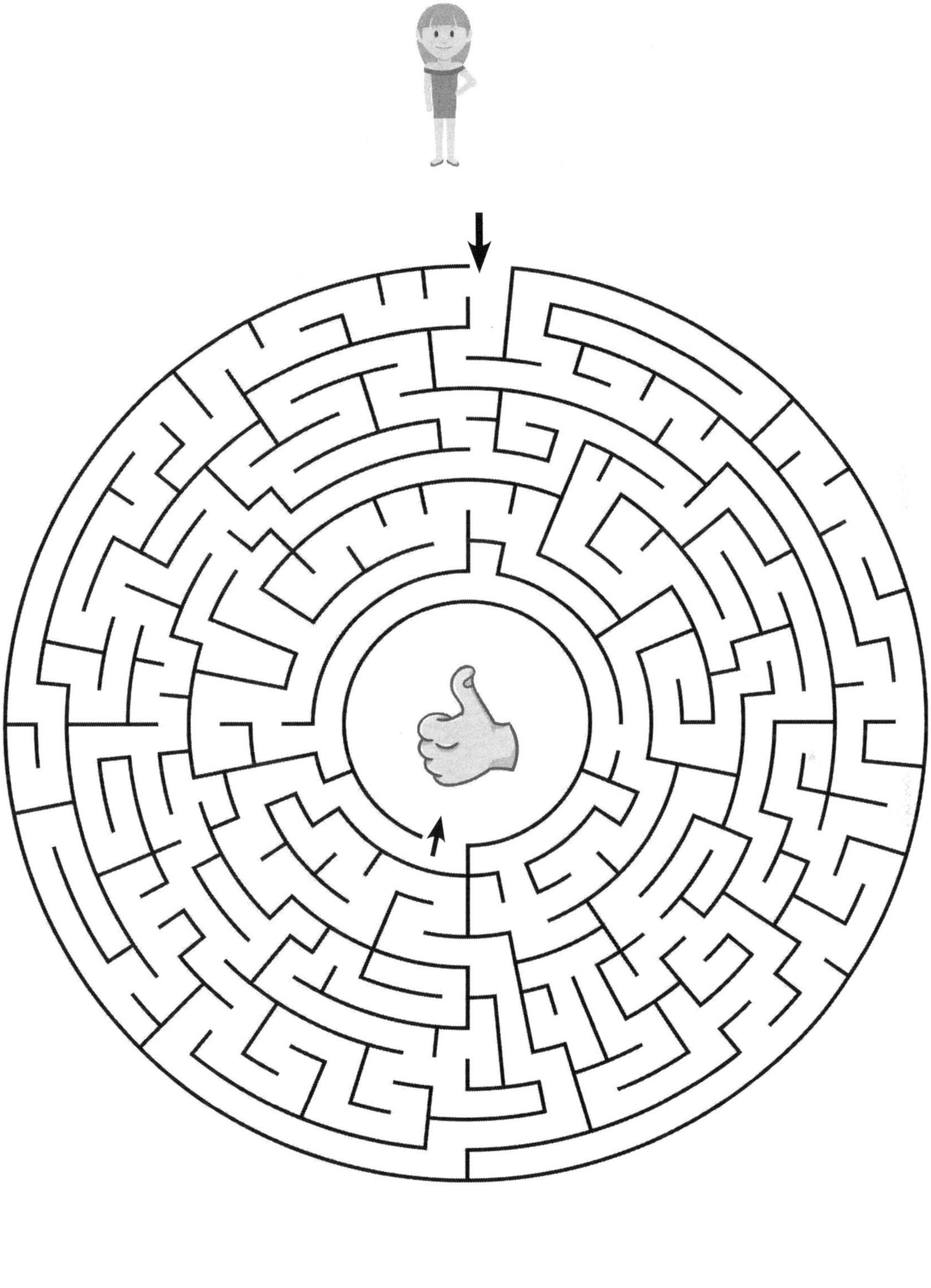

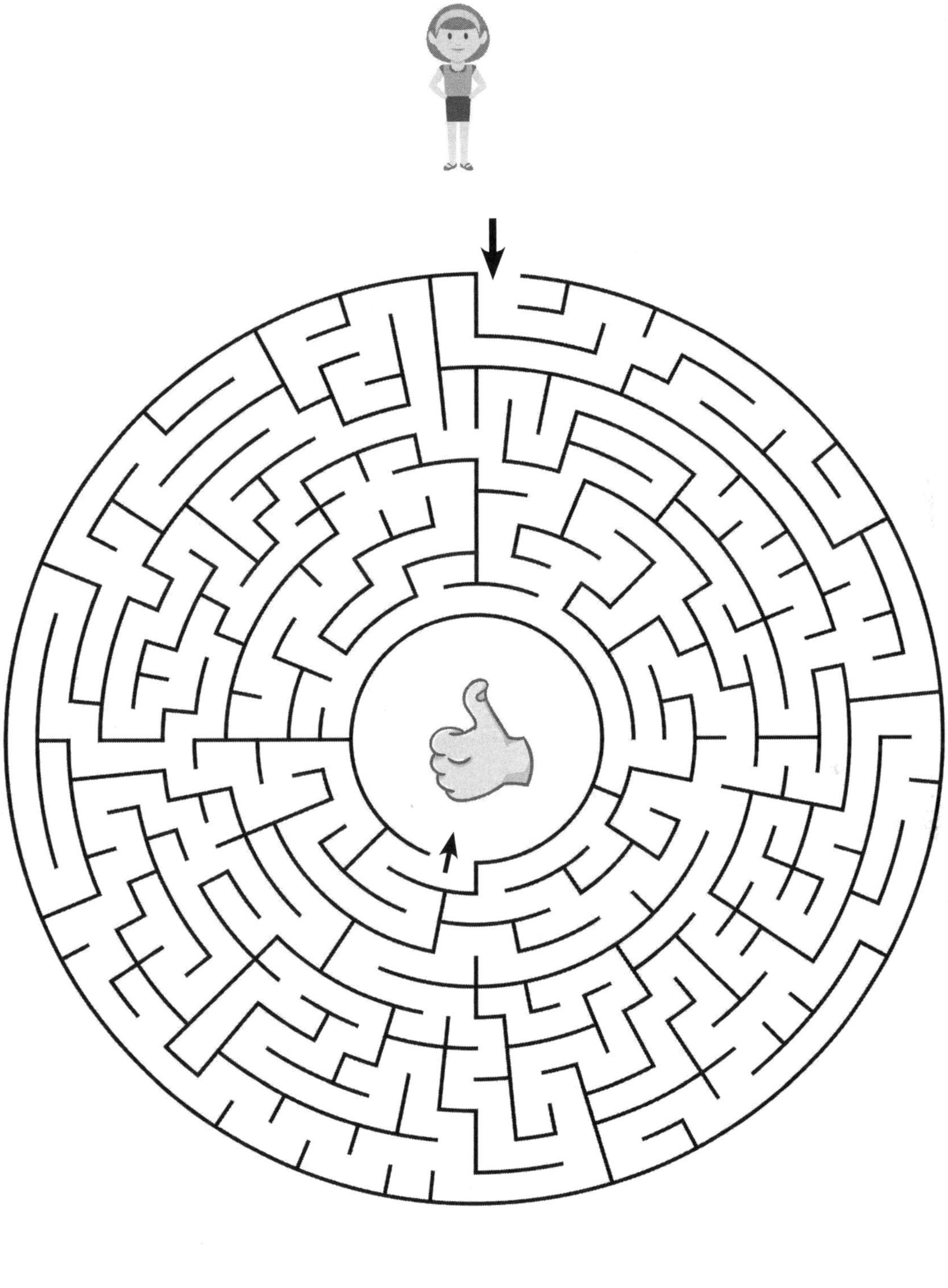

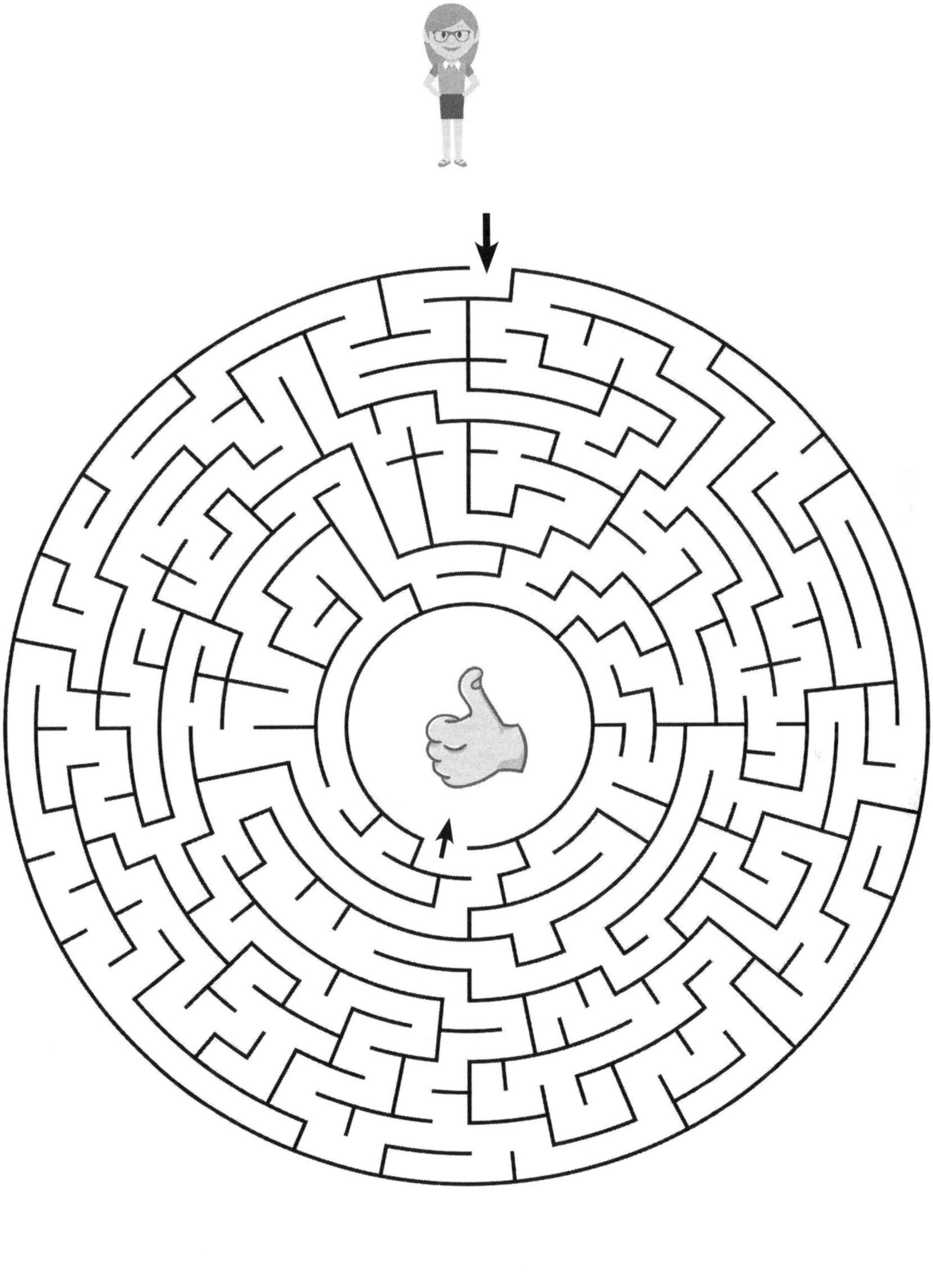

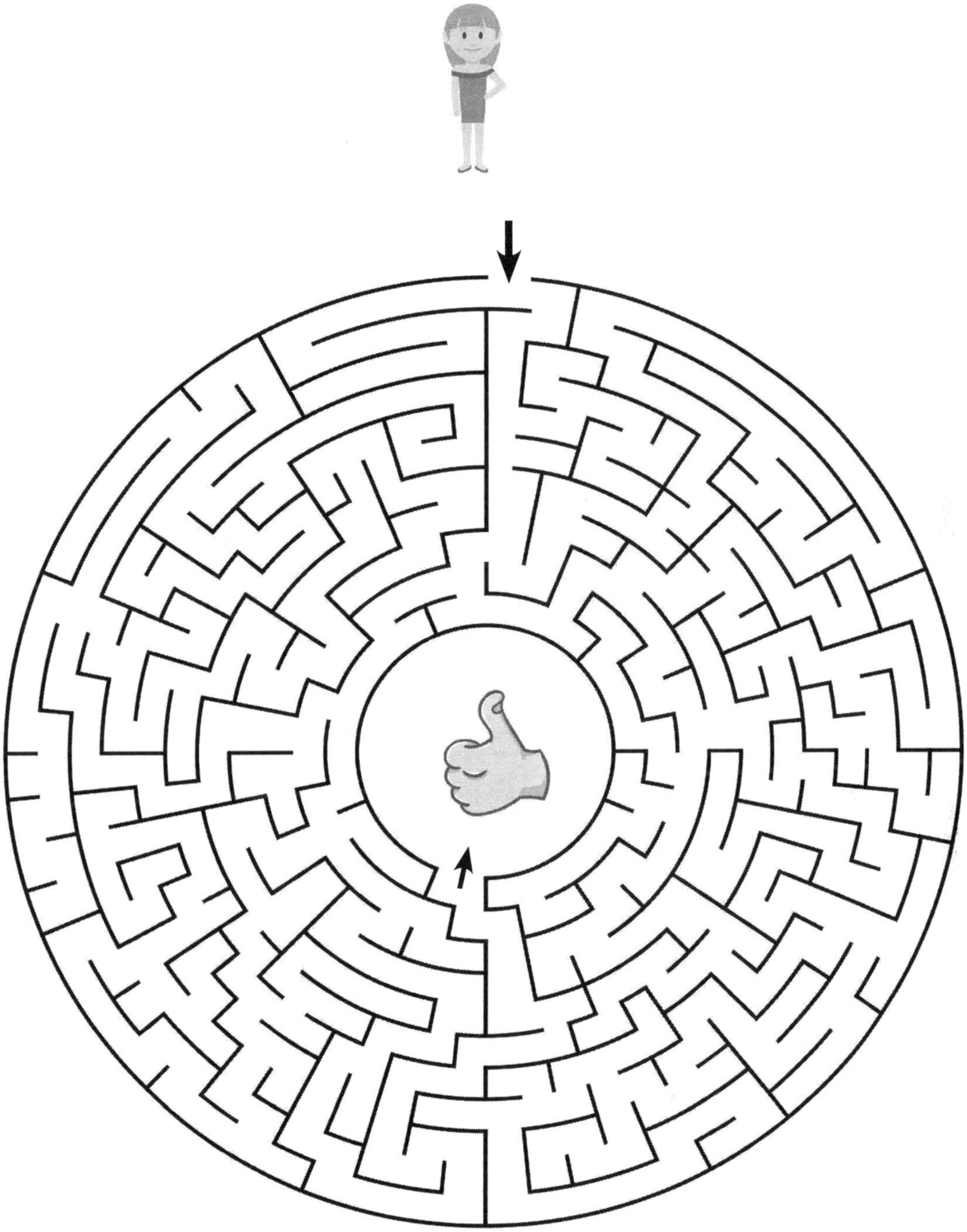

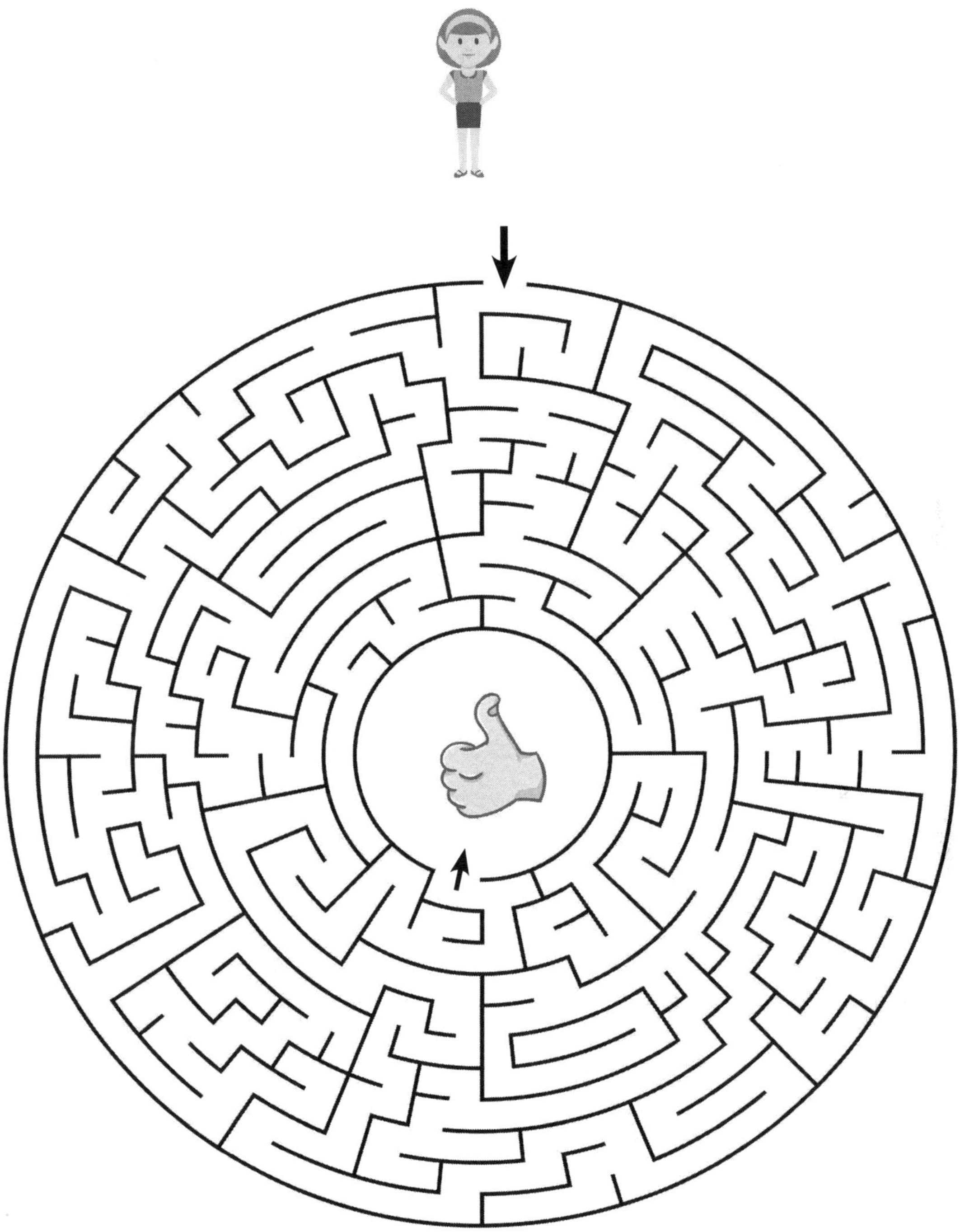

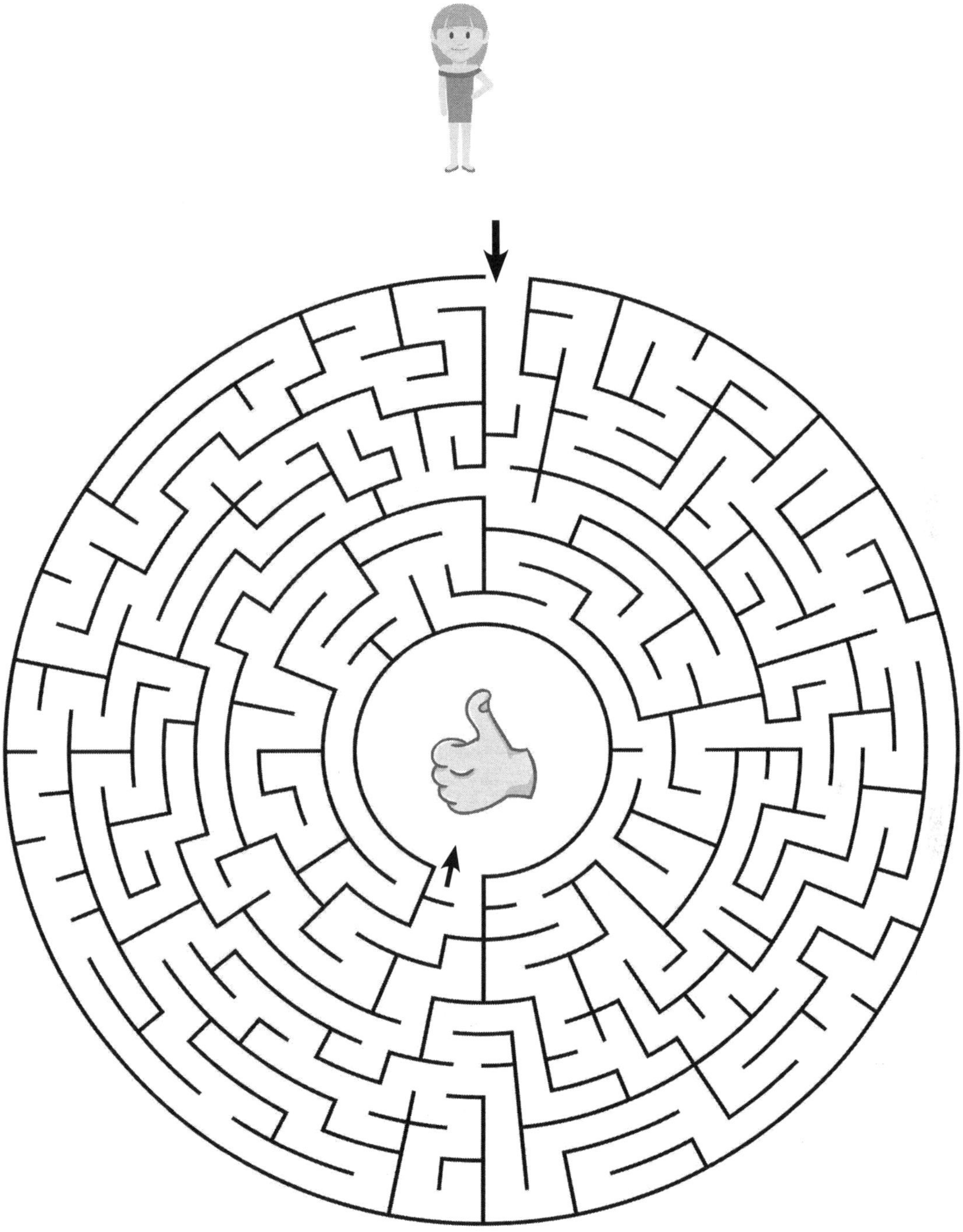

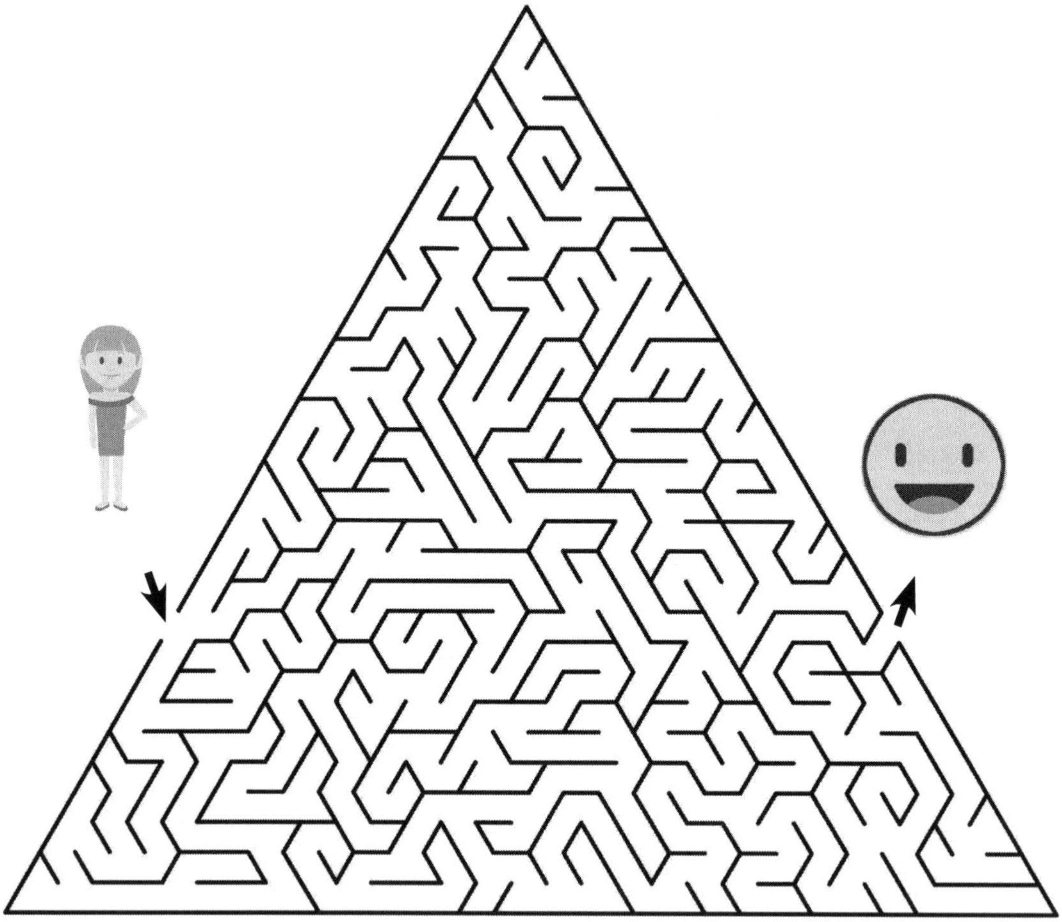

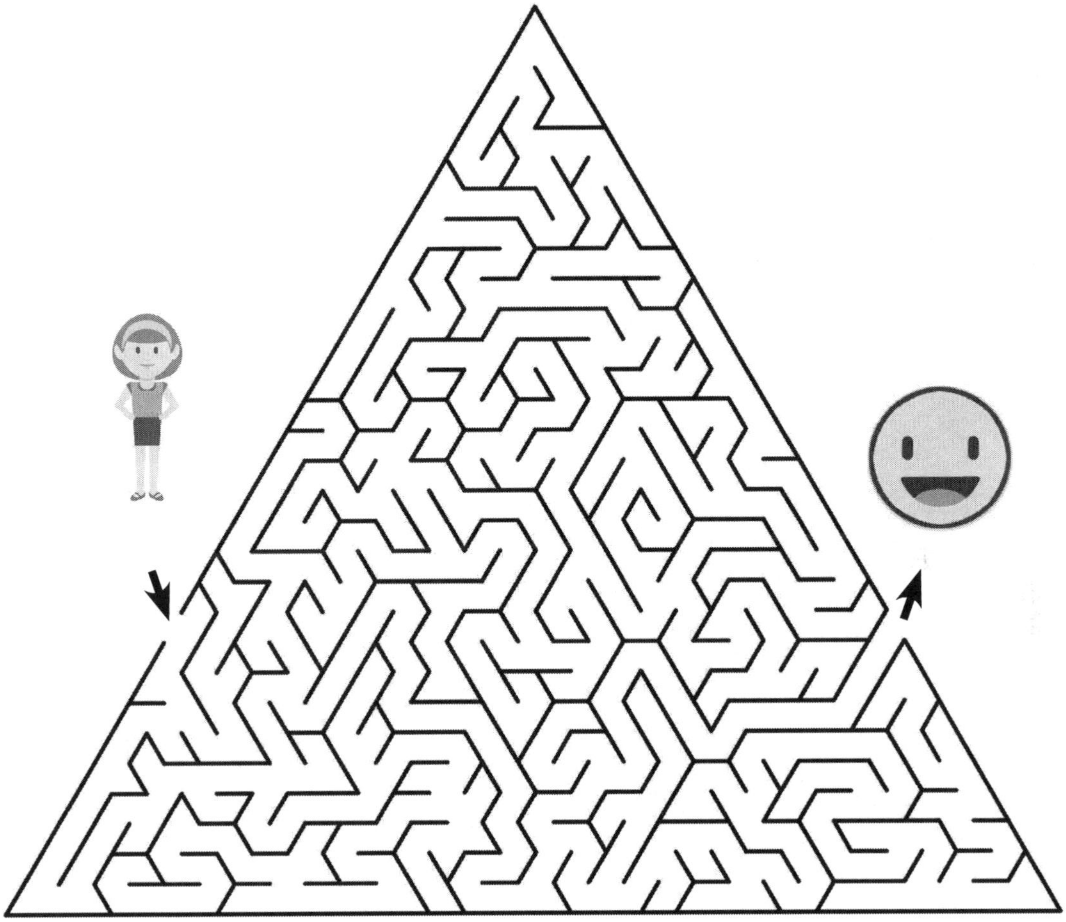

1

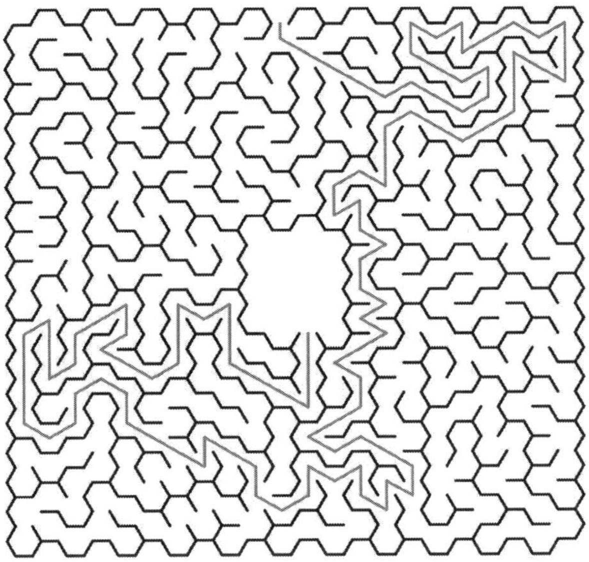

2

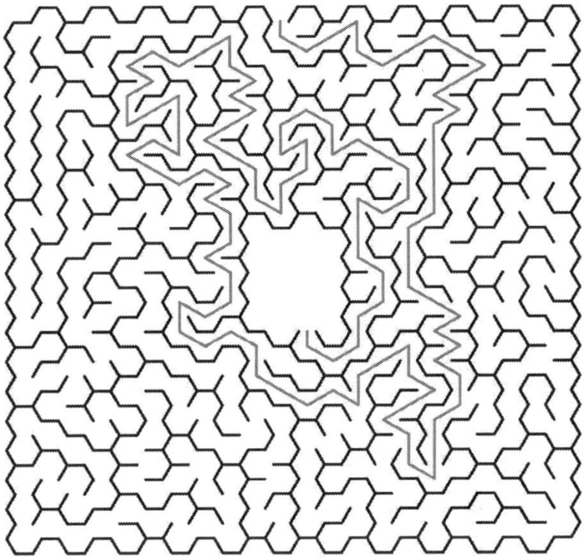

3

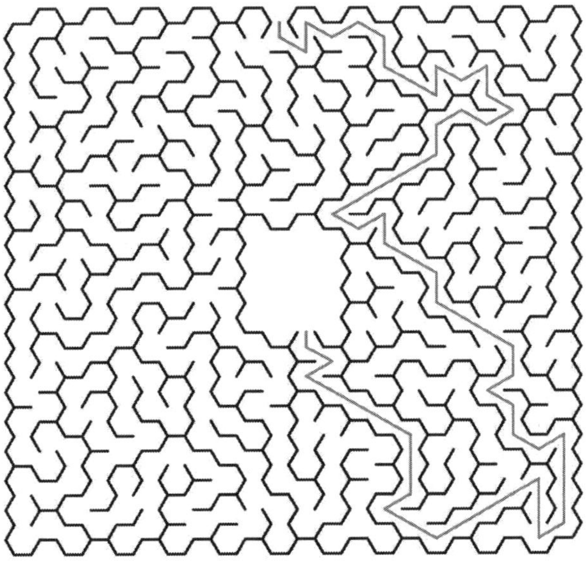

4

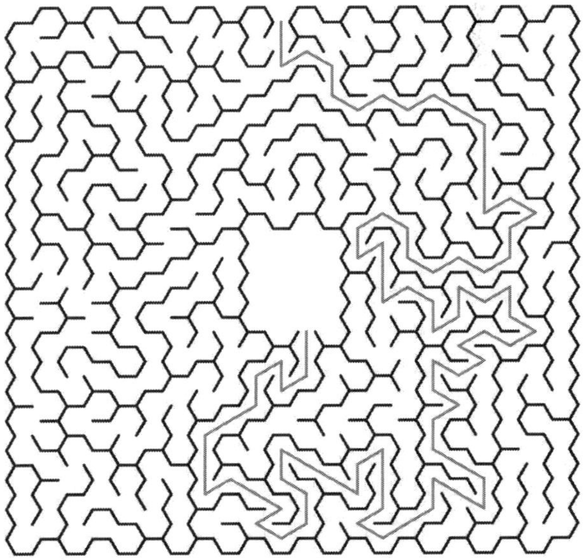

5

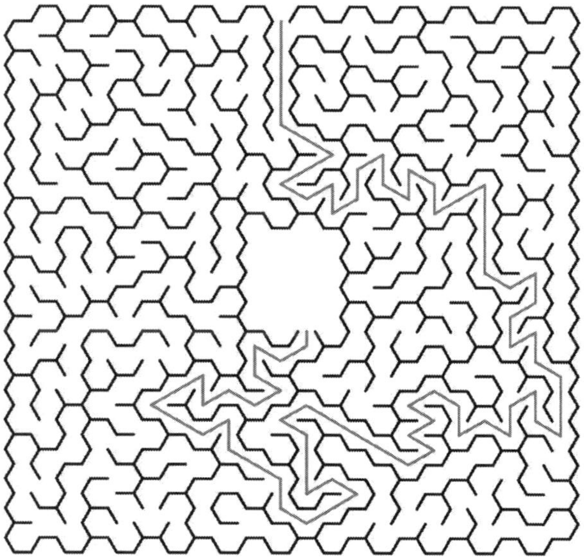

6

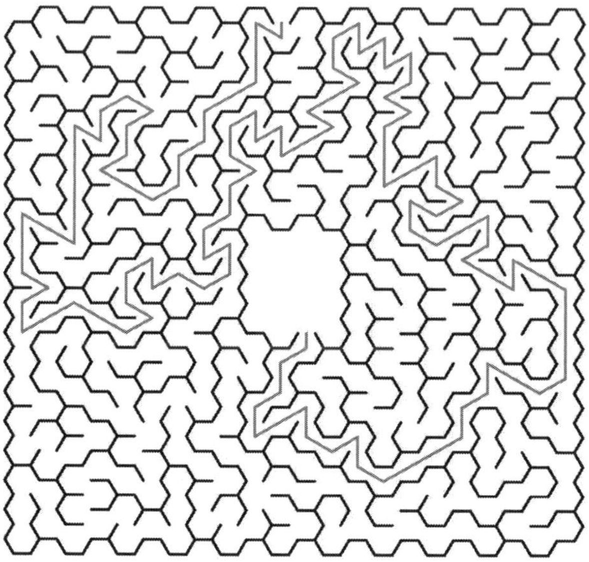

7

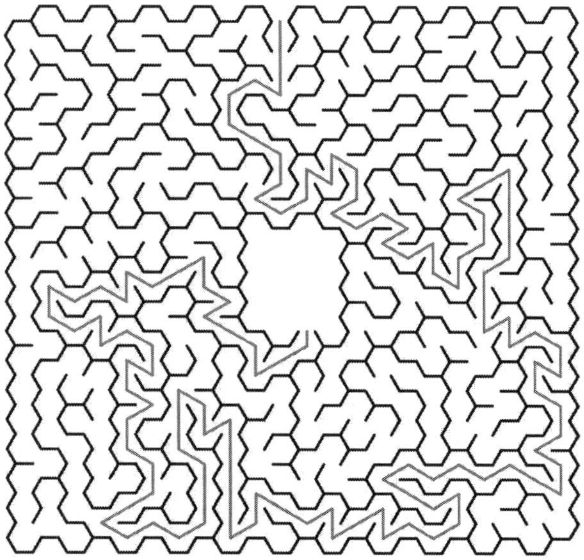

8

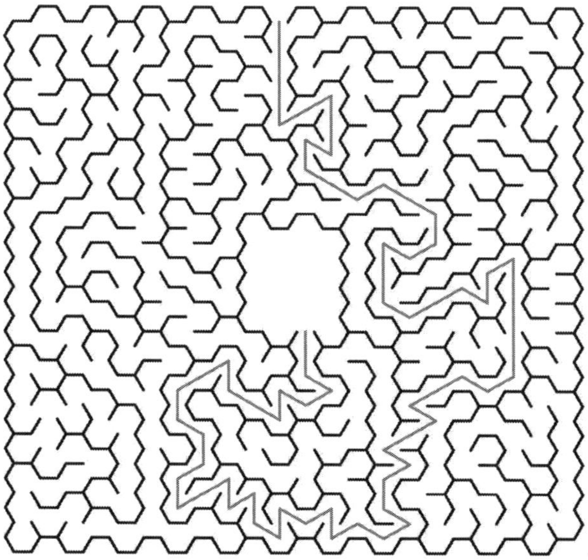

9

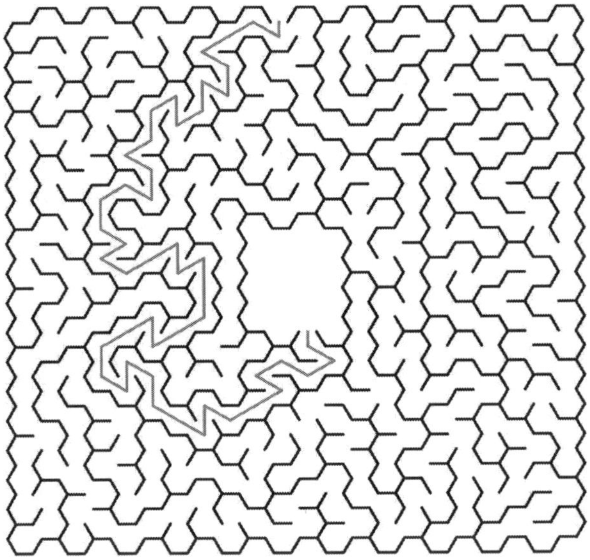

10

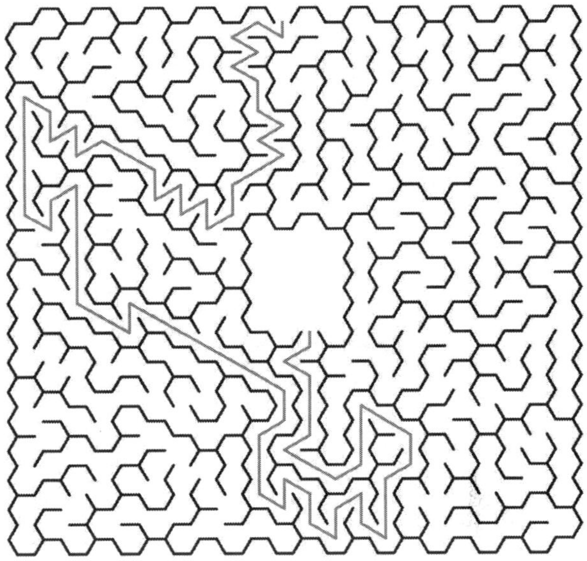

11

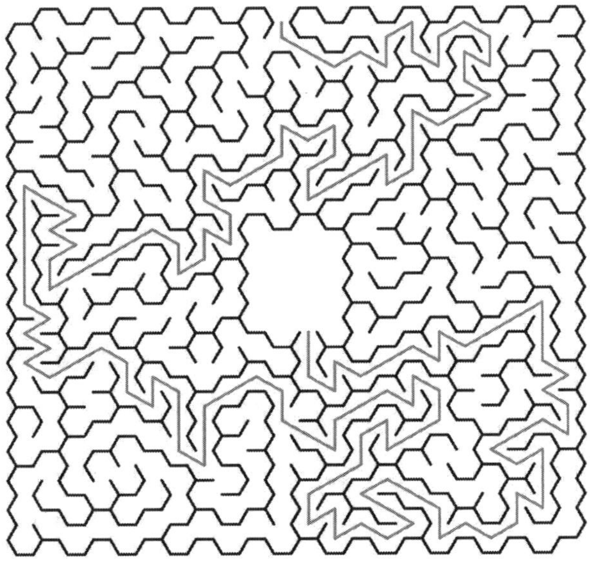

12

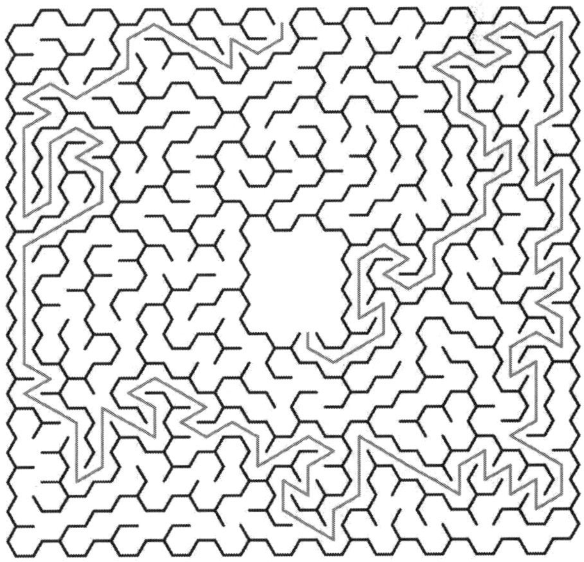

13

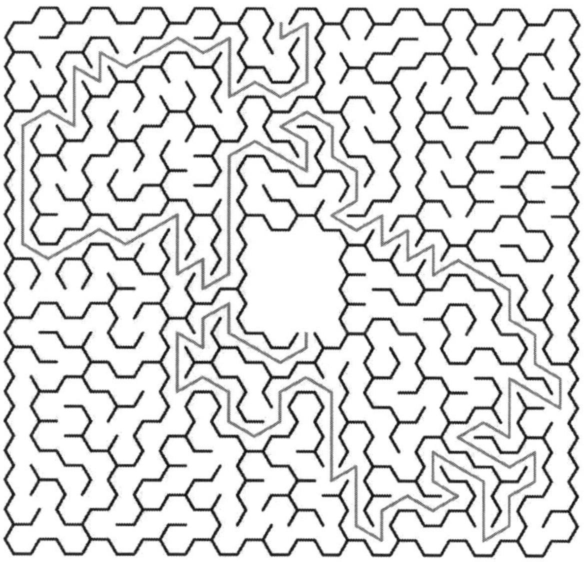

14

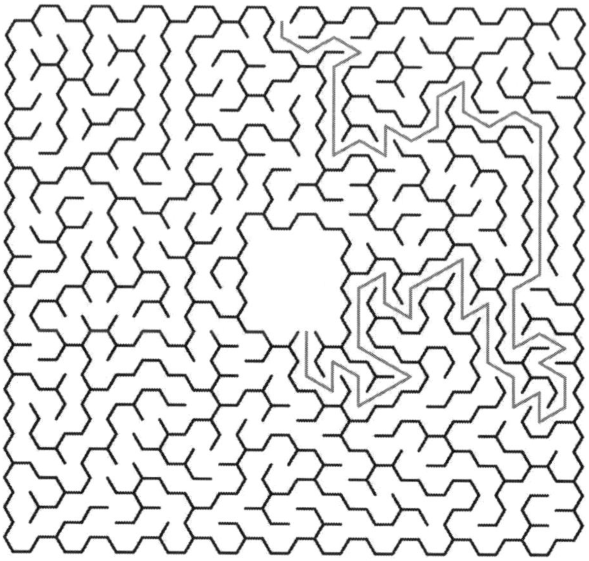

15

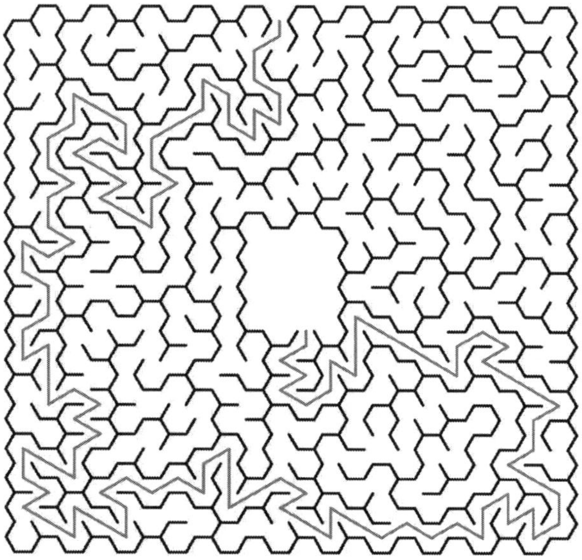

16

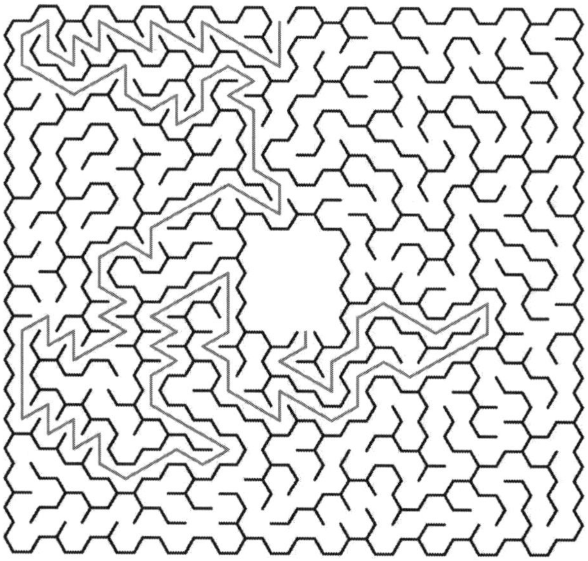

17

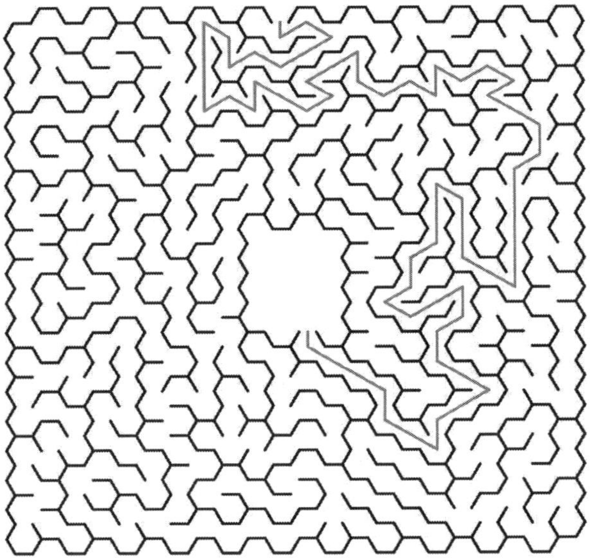

18

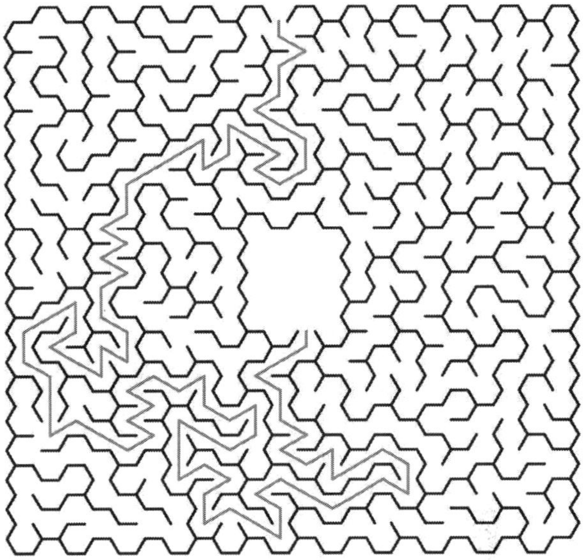

19

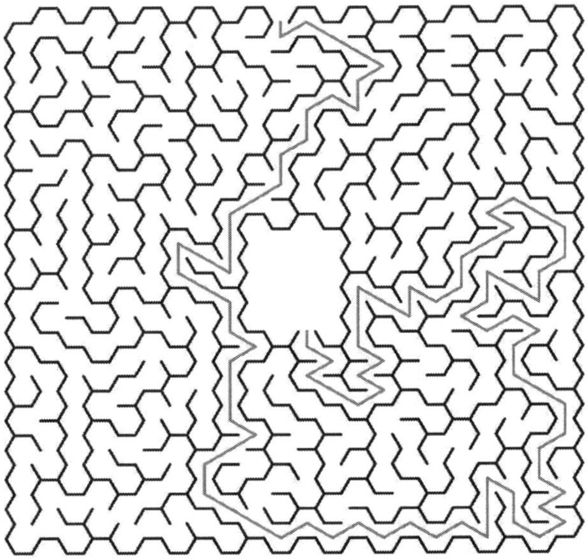

20

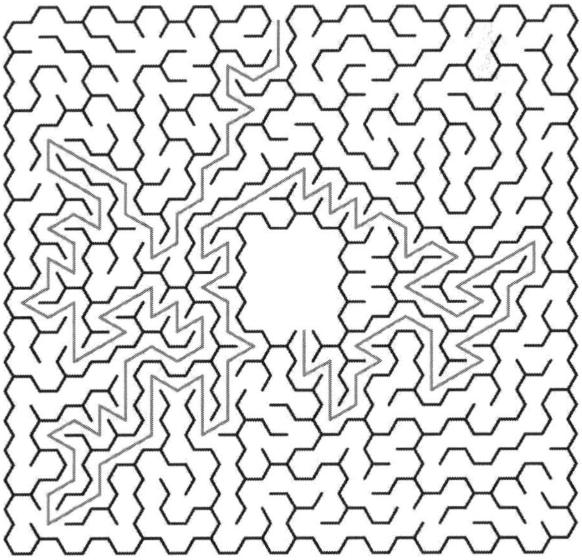

21

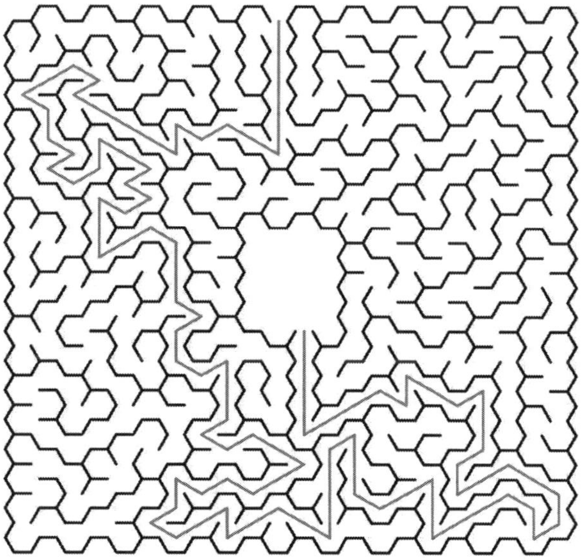

22

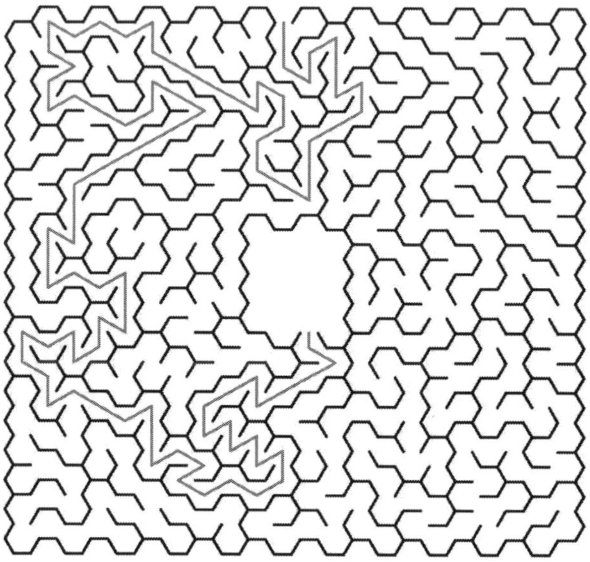

23

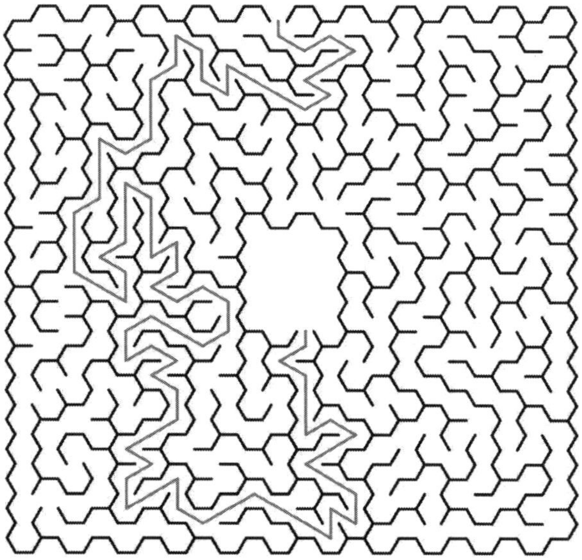

24

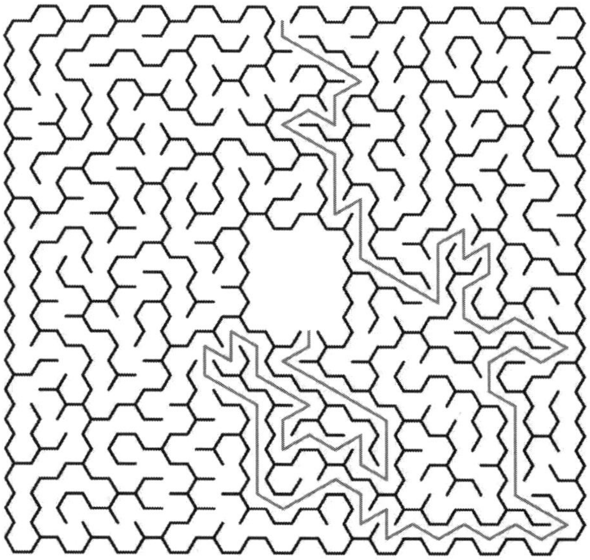

25

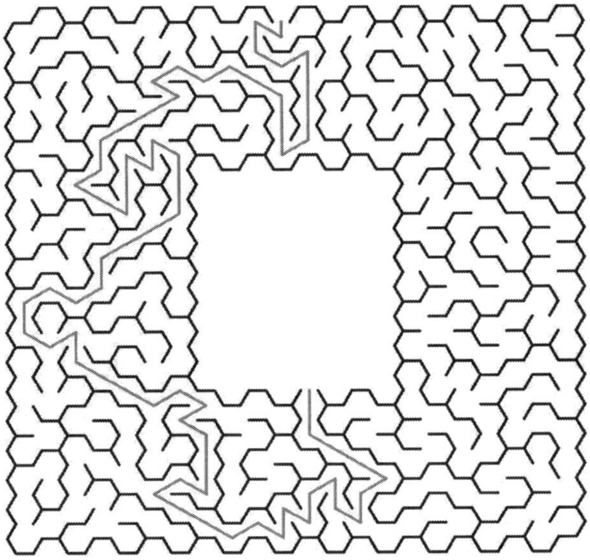

26

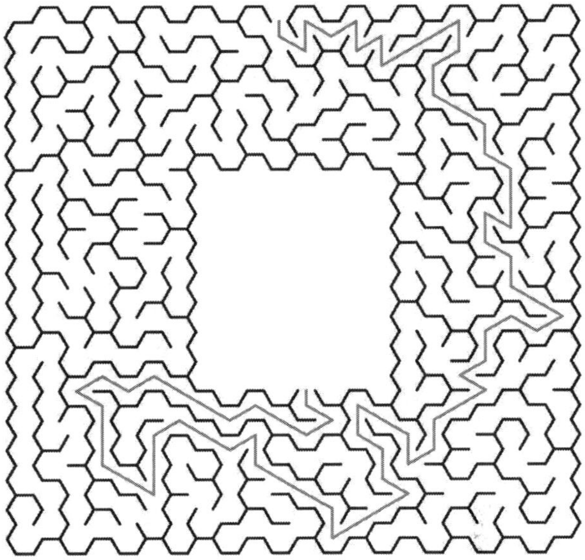

27

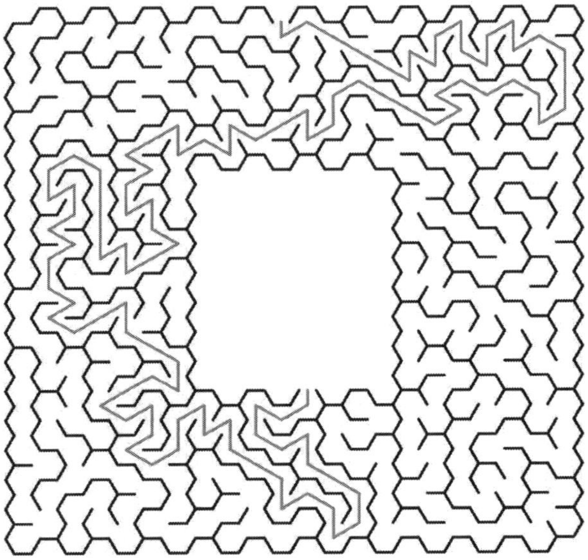

28

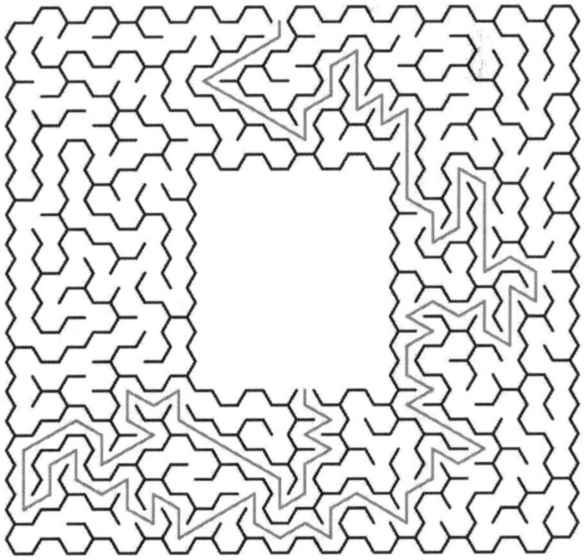

29

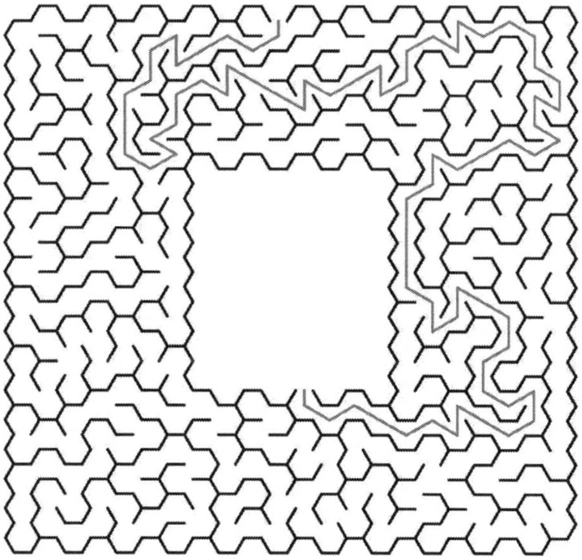

30

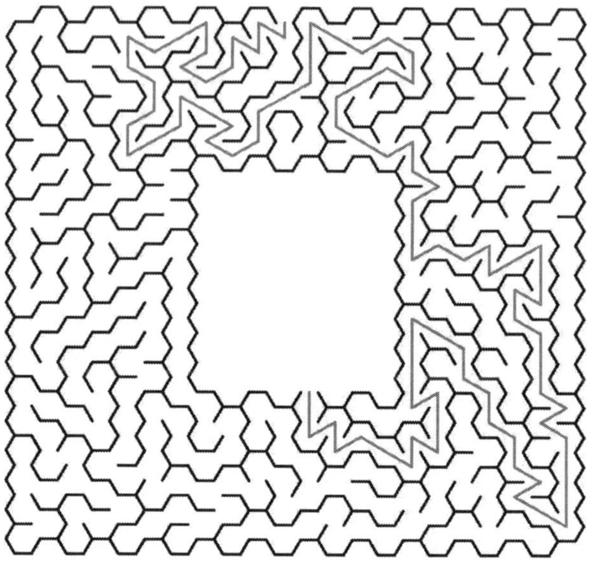

31

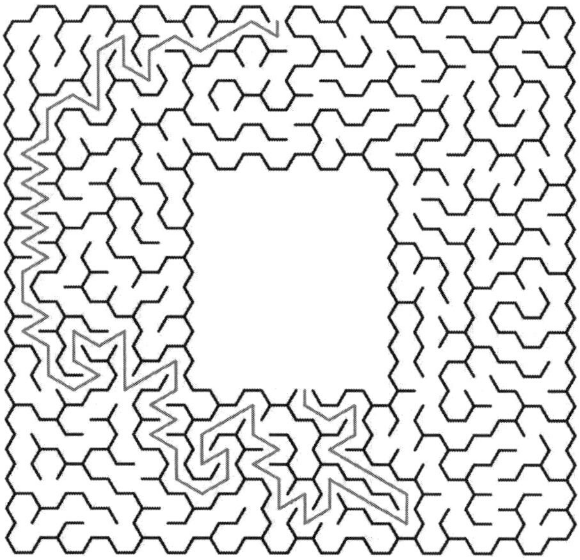

32

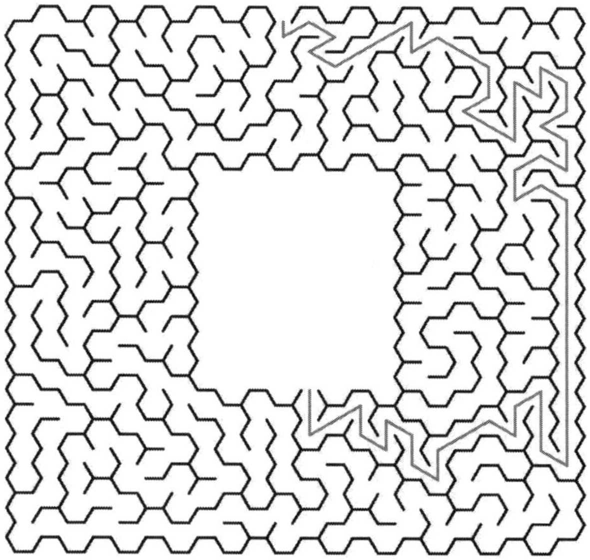

33

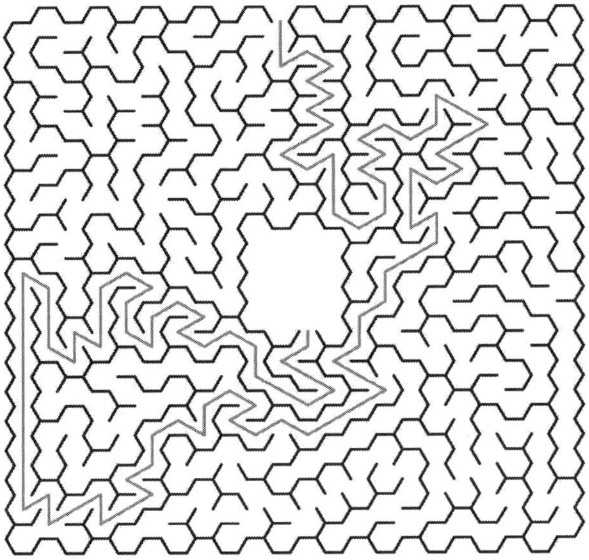

34

35

36

37

38

39

40

41

42

43

44

45

46

47

48

49

50

51

52

53

54

55

56

57

58

59

60

61

62

63

64

65

66

67

68

69

70

71

72

73

74

75

76

77

78

79

80

81

82

Made in the USA
Monee, IL
07 July 2026

56547086R00059